Who do we think we are?

Young Friends' Commitment and Belonging

Swarthmore Lecture 1998

Quaker Home Service

First published in 1998 by
Quaker Home Service
Friends House,
Euston Road,
London
NW1 2BJ

ISBN 0 85245 299 3

Copy editor: Gay Morton
Design and layout: Jonathan Sargent
Printed by Cambrian Printers, Aberystwyth

With thanks to the copyright holders for permission to
include 'Indian Summer' by Dorothy Parker
Extracts from Eleanor Rae 'Women, the Earth, the Divine',
Orbis Books

Preface

The Swarthmore Lectureship was established by the
Woodbrooke Extension Committee at a meeting held
December 9, 1907: the minute of the Committee providing
for an 'annual lecture on some subject relating to the message
and work of the Society of Friends'. The name Swarthmore
was chosen in memory of the home of Margaret Fox, which
was always open to the earnest seeker after Truth, and from
which loving words of sympathy and substantial material help
were sent to fellow workers.

The lectureship has a twofold purpose: first, to interpret
to the members of the Society of Friends their message and
mission; and secondly, to bring before the public the spirit,
the aims and fundamental principles of Friends. The lecturers
alone are responsible for any opinions expressed.

The lectureship provides both for the publication of a
book and for the delivery of a lecture, the latter usually at the
time of assembly of Britain Yearly Meeting of the Society of
Friends. A lecture related to the present book was delivered
at Friends House, Euston Road, London, on the evening of
May 23, 1998.

Foreword

Young Friends General Meeting (YFGM) brings together Quakers and those interested in Quakerism aged 18–30 from all over Britain. We have four or five big gatherings a year, and many smaller groups, local and national, meet frequently to plan events, carry out work on behalf of Young Friends (such as running our appeals, or compiling this book), or simply to spend time together. For many Young Friends, the warm friendship and acceptance they find at these gatherings is very important. In preparing this book, we have gained greatly from the process of loving and honest questioning that we have been through in our search for something to say.

What Quakers share above all is a 'way of doing things', an approach to the spiritual life which is based on the belief that everyone can have direct, personal experience of God. It is that experience, rather than the particular form of words in which it is expressed, that is fundamental to a person's spirituality. We often speak of the need to seek and respond to 'that of God in everyone', referring both to this possibility of personal experience and to the belief that each person has a unique and God-given value.

From these basic ideas come the various aspects of our 'way of doing things'. In our Meetings for Worship, we gather in silence and we try to open ourselves to the love of God and to that of God in each other. Anyone may speak as he or she feels inspired by God to do so. Everyone is equally responsible for the worship; there is no appointed priest or minister, and no predetermined 'order of service'.

Quakers have always emphasised that the whole of life can be lived in response to God, that there is no division between the sacred and the everyday. Our business meetings are conducted in the same spirit and according to the same principles as our Meetings for Worship. We aim to make decisions by a process of collective discernment, considering the issues in silent worship in a co-operative search for the will of God. No votes are taken, since what we seek is not the wishes of the majority, or even simple consensus, but the way forward towards which God is leading us. Many of the decisions taken in writing this book were made in business meetings of Young Friends.

Our belief in 'that of God in everyone' and in the unity of the spiritual life with everyday life has led us, throughout our history, to take stands on many social and political issues, often setting us at odds with the majority of, or the powerful in, society. We have long traditions of opposition to war and of active peacemaking; of concern for the equal treatment of all and of campaigning on behalf of oppressed or excluded groups; and of honesty and truthfulness in all areas of life.

British Quakers today express their spiritual experience in a wide variety of ways. Many would call themselves Christians and use the language and symbols of Christianity; others prefer to find new forms of expression or draw on other faith traditions.

Contents

Openings

It has been said that the future lies with those who will inhabit it — the young. The beliefs and identities of young people provide valuable insight into social change and give an indication as to where society is heading. If this is true for society as a whole, then it is also true for the Religious Society of Friends. However, it must be remembered that the young also inhabit the present. Young Quakers may indicate the future of the Religious Society of Friends, but we are also Quakers of now.

This is a book about Young Friends' attitudes to commitment and belonging, written by a large number of extremely varied individuals. These pages contain a multitude of diverging perspectives and unique reactions, reaching far beyond topics such as marriage or membership. Considering our commitment and belonging in isolation from a whole range of other fundamental issues, such as identity, politics and spirituality, would be a bit like considering a meeting in isolation from the people who make it happen: it would really miss the point. So, as a collection of individual personal testimonies, this book puts commitment and belonging in the context of Young Friends' lives.

A Openings

In the process of considering commitment and belonging and gathering the written testimonies, it became clear that we were focusing on three things: the Religious Society of Friends, our close relationships and our action in the world. (Appendix I describes this in greater detail.) We found that we were addressing some of the most important questions facing us today, both as a Society and as individuals. The experiences described in the contributions bear witness to the central significance of commitment and belonging in all our lives. Perhaps underlying all the contributions is the idea that all expressions of commitment and belonging are valid to those who individually discern and own them.

As our living testimony, we want the book not to be read and put aside, but to become the basis for an interactive process, a 'living' book. Although it has been structured so that it can be read chapter by chapter, from beginning to end, this book is intended to be more adventurous than that. Throughout the book, choices are offered to the reader suggesting alternative pathways, allowing it to be read in a non-linear way. Many questionnaires, workshops and small group sessions have been an integral part of creating this lecture, and some of the material gathered from these events has been used to form signposts at the beginning of each chapter, intended to guide the reader on his or her journey through the book. Further suggestions are given after most of the written contributions, and some challenging questions are included to provoke individual thought.

Many different voices speak in this text. The language may not always be quite what you expect. Some of us have taken to using the spelling 'godde' instead of 'God', pronounced the same, to dissociate the experience of the numinous from the hierarchical and patriarchal image of a 'jealous, vengeful old man in the clouds'. There is a lot of anger and pain in some of the contributions, and we need to be listened to. If you find yourself shocked or annoyed by what you read, take responsibility for your feelings and be prepared to challenge yourself.

The process of considering the themes of commitment and belonging has had a profound effect on the lives of many individual Young Friends, as these contributions attest:

◆ How has being part of writing the Swarthmore Lecture changed my life? Oh, totally. I feel like a different person to who I was a year ago. My whole life has changed. I have moved to the other side of the country, I have a new partner. In this process I have re-evaluated everything I do (to an extent) in the light of the new importance of the issues that have arisen.

◆ I am trying much harder now to do what I believe in, to do what is best for me and my life as well as for my friends, my lover, my relations, in fact anyone I come into contact with. My feelings towards the natural world have been sharpened and I feel more passionate about many things. I get more fired up by things than I have in years, and I feel great about that. I feel now that my feelings are valid, as valid as those of the people I hold respect for and had always thought of as knowing more than I do. I feel that my passions drive what I do and believe.

◆ The process of being closely involved with the 1998 Swarthmore Lecture has made me think very deeply about what is at the heart of Quakerism. It has made me realistic about the Religious Society of Friends. I feel I have had my blinkers removed. I am aware of the Society's limitations and also of its potential. I have applied for membership in a joyful and lucid state ... The process has made me more willing to trust my instincts (what I call 'that of God'). I have begun to 'let go and let God'.

For the most part, contributions to this book have come from those who attend Young Friends General Meeting, the national body of young adult Quakers (18+) in Britain. The following extracts from Minute 97/14 of YFGM best describe the process we have been through as a group:

> In February 1996, YFGM accepted an invitation to give the 1998 Swarthmore Lecture on the themes of Commitment and Belonging. Although we were aware it was a massive undertaking, we were unaware of the impact it would have on us as individuals and as a Meeting for Worship. The Steering Group accepted the onerous job of clarifying the task ahead. Sometimes they have had an uphill struggle convincing us of the importance, potential and enormity of what we had agreed to do. After much hard work, discussions and workshops, a group of 15 Young Friends met in January 1997 to draft a synopsis of the book, which provides a framework for the publication. During that weekend, it became clear that the process we as a meeting were going through was affecting us deeply as individuals.
>
> Thinking about what we mean by commitment and belonging has drawn us together as a worshipping community. It has also affected us as individuals. For some, it has prompted applications of membership to the Religious Society of Friends. For others, a clarification of areas of their lives. What is clear for any Young Friend who has been involved with the process, at any stage, whether it be by writing, discussing, or worshipping, the words 'commitment' and 'belonging' are no longer just two words...
>
> ...Through creative listening in small groups, we examined what limits us – as Quakers and as Young Friends – and what distinguishes us from other groups of young people. We have been encouraged and helped to

write contributions by those present at the Synopsis Drafting weekend. Many Friends have shared with the Meeting their personal experience of the effect the process has had on their lives. It has been very moving for all of us to take part in...

Some of us have also had a nagging question. We were asked as Young Friends General Meeting in Britain to consider the issues surrounding commitment and belonging. Why? Perhaps the most obvious, innocent answer is that those that asked us believed Young Friends might have a different and interesting perspective on some of the most pressing and acute problems that face our Society (of Friends) and our society (more generally). Some traditional expressions of commitment, such as marriage, are being challenged as the values of society in general are shifting. Whenever there is radical change in such sacred institutions as the family, people want to know why and get an idea of where we may be going.

The conspiracy theorists amongst us, though, see a hidden agenda. Young Friends have obviously strayed, like so many prodigal daughters and sons. Why not give them a task that distracts them, keeps them out of trouble and forces them to consider the error of their ways? What better way of getting them to take up the traditional commitments than to get them to work hard at considering those very commitments and their responses to them? If those damn young Quakers don't wake up to their responsibilities this way, they'll never do it.

Whatever the truth, it worked! The business of Young Friends has been so clogged up with considering commitment and belonging in every possible permutation and combination that we have managed to forget about nuclear weapons, road building, the Criminal Justice Act, and even Abkhazia, at least for some of the time. We have sat in considered silence, contemplating our convictions, our priorities, our faith. In worship, discussion, painting, role-play, human sculpture – you name it – we've been engrossed, actively exploring our identities. Now it's time to share it – who do we think we are? Read on...

I am committed to doing what feels right for me and finding my way spiritually. 'Feeling right' is about a sense of peace and trust and joy in my life but not necessarily ease. It's about finding out who I am at the deepest level.

*Do you feel you are doing what feels right for you? Try **B9**.*

My spiritual path is my relationship with my windspirit. A complete unknown, but not at all frightening. All the words that I think of don't seem to apply.

*Is this the same as being inexpressible, as in **B7**?*

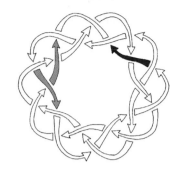

Paths and Definitions

How would you describe the spiritual/religious path to which you are committed?

I am not committed to any one spiritual path. I have a general desire to become more enlightened, by whatever path seems best at the time. The goal includes personal development and the development of abilities to help other people.

Is this what the writer of **B2** *is describing?*

I feel a sense of belonging that can probably be described as 'sharing my spiritual path with others'. My commitment is to discovering the divine (or God, or Buddha…) within myself and others.

Quakerism can provide the space to do this, see **B1**.

B Paths and Definitions

B1 Why am I a Quaker? Sometimes, I am transformed by a powerful force. It has unrelentingly dragged me shaking to my feet in Meeting for Worship as I burn with something to say; it has held me as I walk through a still avenue of huge sycamore trees, worrying about a family member who has just been admitted to hospital; it has filled me with joy as I contemplate a vista of sky and landscape from the top of a mountain; it has been present between me and my partner after making love, as we lie in a kind of timeless intimacy. Sometimes I feel centred and moved by something beyond my own experience. It is a kind of force which prompts me, prompts my conscience, my emotions, my desires.

Quakers give me the space to seek that force in myself and in others, to come to know it, to test it, to act upon it. Quakers give me that space unconditionally. I can explore it by being just me, and I feel valued for who I am. That is why I belong.

For another description of experiences in Meeting for Worship, see **F6**.

What makes us feel we belong? Turn to **C1**.

See **F. Discernment and Worship**.

B2 Commitment to Quakerism seems almost to be commitment to vagueness, a commitment to being non-committal on questions of belief. Is that why so many people are attracted to the Society – because it's easy to belong here? Within Quakerism, what does it mean to be spiritually committed? How is it possible to be committed to what we can't express, for fear of reducing it to ourselves or giving the wrong impression to others? If I'm asked the equivalent of 'What canst thou say?', it often seems best to answer 'Er… nothing really…'. If that's the case, what is our commitment worth? Friends often seem to talk about the 'commitment to seeking', and it's probably worth exploring further.

Our most important commitments are always inexpressible. I

cannot tell you why she is my friend. I could talk about specific things we have in common, or times we enjoy together, but that would not be an explanation. Nor can I tell what she is like so that you would know her as she is in her uniqueness. I could not show you a photograph which would let you see her face as I see it. Nor can I explain fully what actions or attitudes of mine constitute friendship. The more time I spend with her and the better I get to know her, the less of her and the less of our friendship I can express. Similarly, when I begin to talk about what I take to be my moral 'commitments', there comes a point beyond which I cannot go in giving reasons.

Intangible? Perhaps, but worth more for that reason. Worth more to me than the definition of friendship in a dictionary, or the best-argued ethical theory. And still worth talking about, despite the failure of words to encompass it.

Do we at least have to try to express our spiritual lives, even though we may believe that they are ultimately inexpressible in words?

You may like to compare this paragraph with **E16**.

B3   Commitment can be a shackle or a support. It can be a process of sanctification or a grinding toil. I prefer to see my commitment to living a spiritual life as a member of the Religious Society of Friends as an enriching one. I made a commitment to myself last summer that I would recite to myself a piece of 'spiritual writing' upon waking each morning. I found that this simple commitment, to a particular ritual way of starting the day, helps to ground me in my life as an expression of godde's will.

B4   How would we define godde? Often, when I am trying to give an overview of Quakerism to a new friend or acquaintance when they discover I am a Quaker, I find myself in the middle of my description of godde (or what this term means to me), and wonder whether I am fooling myself with my rehearsed idea of godde and whether I am actually a total non-believer.

B5   I believe that I was made the way I was, with my talents, for a purpose. I try to follow my 'bliss' – what is deeply enjoyable to me – because I see it as a path leading to what godde intends me to do. I find that deep fulfilling happiness comes to me through exercising a skill beautifully, making art that is useful, wherever it is.

B6   There is frequently an expression of commitment to the process of seeking and discernment. The danger is that we become attached to the state of limbo, which prevents us from nailing the colours to the mast. Commitment requires time and energy, often without clear certainty. It has been said that what aids the process of commitment is trust, letting go of our fierce independence, and approaching our lives with a certain humility. Prayer and meditation are powerful tools for positive action… as are songs and other forms of creative expression.

Is there any point to action anyway? See **M11**.

If we are committed to seeking, does that mean we do nothing?
See **N19**.

B7   Maybe I should say nothing at all about what I know and am committed to, since nothing can express it. If we cannot say anything, why not remain silent? Even in traditions not so centred on silence as Quakerism, there has always been a strong awareness of the risks we take as soon as we begin to speak about God. Judaism, of course, has the 'Name of the Name' that cannot be spoken; every discussion of Christian theology uses 'negative theology', talk of God which proceeds by saying only what God is not. Can I commit myself to saying something that I know to be inadequate? Is it not better to commit myself to saying nothing?

When I talk to someone about a deep feeling or a new idea, I am aware that my words are conveying very little of what is in my mind. I am aware that they are open to misinterpretation and that I have no way of knowing how they are understood. I take a risk in trying to put anything into words.

*The writer of **F12** isn't sure what words should be used either.*

B8 Language is a constant challenge for Quakers and we seem to be obsessed about it, in our minor corrections to minutes, in our labels of 'Christocentric' and 'universalist', 'corporatist' and 'grass roots'.

Language is the interpretation of an experience, the signifier, the expression of something greater. Interpretation is essential, because we are committed to a truthful representation of our promptings – a life of integrity. However, sometimes interpretation of the experience, rather than the experience of the prompting itself, can become the absorbing matter. Sometimes I feel the interpretation of the prompting – the values and culture of the Religious Society of Friends – is all people are committed to, and we lose sight of our inner core.

I am committed to Quakerism and to the way we live our lives as Quakers, but the expressions of our faith amongst ourselves – our attitude to labels, our obsession with processes and our self-maintenance – sometimes make me shuffle and twitch, and question whether I do really belong.

*Try **E15** or **E17** for different thoughts on the way our*
spirituality is expressed.

B9 When I talk about my career, I tend to get all fired up with ideas about where I want to go and what I want to do. I set myself goals all the time. Some of them are complete fantasies, about communicating on a massive scale – a concert, or television; some are more realistic, and I do actually get there. I'll be doing something pretty normal, like talking to some friends about where politics is going while sitting in a cosy café, and I'll stop and think to myself, 'hey, I'm so lucky – I'm happy, and I'm doing what I want to do, and maybe I'm taking my time, but I'm going in the right direction for me'.

Do actions speak louder than feelings? The writer of **N21** *also reminds us to look to where we are now.*

Do you make these momentary connections?
Read what **N22** *has to say.*

B10 Icebergs are HUGE. They are sparkling white, beautiful, holding a strong attraction. But we can't see most of them, because they're also dark and murky, hidden from view. And they're bloody scary. We're afraid of dashing ourselves against them. Losing ourselves... A bit like commitment. A bit like love too.

Consider the SS Religious Society of Friends. A great bulk of a ship that requires discipline and a structured hierarchy to keep it afloat. But it's sinking by its very weight, after striking against the sharp edges of the commitment iceberg.

Each generation needs to find its own way through the iceberg floes. The icebergs are treacherous, but they also hold the key to life.

What kind of discipline do we need? Is it the discipline of following a path that has been shown, or the fortitude to stay with an example that teaches us to forge our own paths? Look at **F9**.

K4 *looks at changes through generations.*

B11

A friend of mine once said to me,
'So what do Quakers do?
Wear black hats and quake a lot:
That doesn't seem like you!'

My efforts to describe to her,
I fear, did not explain
Exactly what it means to me, so
Here I go again...

It's a feeling of belonging,
It's standing on one's own,
It's shouting out together,
It's speaking all alone.
    It's knowing we are all unique,
    With thoughts, desires and fears,
    It's sharing our emotions,
    It's laughter and it's tears.
It's freedom to and freedom from,
It's freedom to be me,
It lets me be just who I am,
It sets my spirit free.
    It's joyfulness and laughter,
    It's sadness and remorse,
    It's passivity and letting go,
    It's power and it's force.
It's love and understanding,
It's joy, respect and awe,
It's something deep inside my heart,
Within my very core.

We're all of us on journeys;
The destination is unknown.
Our paths may sometimes intertwine,
Sometimes we tread alone.

It's there to support us,
To light the darkened way.
We see the light in others
In spectacular array.

(I fear this answer baffled her
As all she said was 'Cor'.
I felt I should say one more thing,
'It's all of that... and more.')

23

C   Membership

Yes, I belong and I intend to become a member at a point when I am in one place long enough to become closely involved with the life of one preparative meeting (PM). I belong to the Religious Society of Friends because I am at home – spiritually, socially, whatever.

Membership is a responsibility, not just a label. See **C2**.

No, I am not a member, but I am very involved in Young Friends General Meeting and am satisfied that I belong here. I am loosely attached to the Religious Society of Friends in that I go to meeting.

Does being inward looking stop us looking outward? Try **C8**.

Membership

Do you feel you belong to the Religious Society of Friends?
How would you describe this belonging?

I belong in the sense that my local meeting has welcomed and accepted me, despite a generation gap. This 'belonging' is not espccially strong, but it's there and is probably growing with time and with effort and conversation.

*See **C5** for something similar.*

*The writer of **C9** had a more uncomfortable experience and gave up. Should they have persevered?*

Yes, a home. A buzz. New experience. Spiritual experience. Connections I want to work at. A resource. A support. An identity.

*Is this the same as 'magic'? See **C13**.*

C Membership

C1 Many of us would become members if we could feel part of a monthly meeting, but there are five obstacles to this type of belonging. First, most of us change addresses frequently throughout our twenties. Second, partly as a result of this itineracy, many of us have contacts and commitments all over the country that can take us away from base at weekends. Third, few of us are raising families, which would provide some stability as well as making our presence at meeting more obvious. Fourth, some meetings, while good at welcoming newcomers, seem to have trouble realising when a newcomer has become part of them: many Young Friends have been through the experience of being welcomed to a meeting they have attended regularly for months. Lastly, it is often retired Friends who have time to take on responsibility within a meeting. The moment when one becomes a member of the Religious Society of Friends is not necessarily the same as the moment when one becomes committed to it.

C2 The issue of membership is often raised in the Religious Society of Friends: what is the difference between a member and an attender? Does the distinction matter? Membership, at least when based on the technical definition, may appear as a passport to an assortment of meetings and positions, allowing participation at a higher level. However, a reversal of this perspective gives a more realistic view. Membership is not an acquisition of rights but an acceptance of responsibilities, and is fundamentally a religious commitment.

Membership can be seen as an outward manifestation of both our commitment and our belonging to the Religious Society of Friends. Whereas an attender may be committed to only a fraction of the life and work of the Society – for example, a local Meeting for Worship or Young Friends General Meeting – membership implies commitment at and to all levels. A member cannot regard any section of the Society as a group to which they have no responsibility or commitment. So as I see it, no member should refer to Yearly Meeting as 'them'; it is fundamentally composed of 'us'.

This statement of commitment is made not only to yourself but to your monthly meeting and to the Society as a whole. It is because membership matters that the process of application is and should be a serious and meaningful undertaking, not a mere formality. This is my understanding of the meaning of membership of the Religious Society of Friends.

However, I feel that this understanding is not necessarily shared or appreciated throughout the Society. For example, it is often easy for a child of a Quaker family to attain membership almost by default. It should not be assumed that a person who has been known to the meeting for most of their life is necessarily well equipped for membership. Rather, I feel that the process of gaining membership requires more active participation and consideration by both the applicant and the meeting.

There is also a danger that any member may feel their commitment lies solely with the local meeting rather than with the wider Society. This is visible, for example, in low attendance at monthly meetings and an unwillingness to acknowledge ownership of corporate work.

Finally, the misunderstanding of membership is closely linked to a failure to address the central role of religion in the Religious Society of Friends. I value the celebration of diversity of religious understanding in the Society as one of its greatest strengths. My fear is that a reluctance to approach this diversity leads to an unwillingness to express any religious understanding at all. Such timidity can only be damaging. My commitment as a member entails embracing all aspects of the Religious Society of Friends, even those with which I as an individual feel unable to be in unity. Membership of the Religious Society of Friends is the entrusting of my commitment to the wider corporate body to which we belong.

The writer of **F9** *has doubts about the effectiveness of some aspects.*

C3   Young Friends were having a meal together last night and we got talking about the Swarthmore Lecture.

C   Membership

'And you know, there are a staggering number of the synopsis group who've chosen to become members since they got involved with the Swarthmore Lecture.'

I looked over to the most recently 'convinced' Young Friend among us, who was also on the synopsis group. 'Are you a member?'

'I've just applied.'

I went round the table and asked. All six of us were members. At least half were members here, where we are at university. The oldest of us was 23, the youngest, 18.

Suddenly, I felt excluded. Rather than feeling more involved with the Society since musing on the 'Commitment and Belonging' themes (for about the past year), I've become increasingly dissatisfied. My membership, of my home meeting, feels secure, but like a slightly useless ornament: I don't invest anything in that community, much as I love it. There is little point in transferring my membership. I leave university in three months, and I don't know where I'll 'belong' after that. And if so many people have been affected so positively by the Swarthmore Lecture process and I haven't, do I belong in Young Friends General Meeting? I feel envious of their involvement, of their sense of purpose. Why don't I feel as empowered as them, or so included?

Realistically, I have excluded myself. Other priorities, such as my degree and my commitments in the town where I study, have taken precedence. To belong takes work and time. It's also not easy to belong when you have doubts. I keep wanting Quakers to change, sharpen up, improve, become, oh, so incredibly spiritual and active – a utopia i.e. inconceivable, impossible, unattainable, glorious. My feelings of unease about membership rest on a dissatisfaction with the Quaker business method, which I see as the paradigmatic expression of our faith. And so it reaches the point where the question hangs, 'shall I change it from within? Or get out?'

I think back to when I applied for membership. In my year out between school and university, I immersed myself in Quaker communities: at a Quaker guest house, on a US Quaker camp, and in a

Friends centre. On the other side of the world, I heard one Friend say to an attender, 'You already *are* a member. You just haven't written the letter yet. And what's a letter?' That was how I felt – I was a part of Quakerism, the world-wide family of Friends. I already belonged. However, membership still seemed a big step, so I counselled myself towards caution. I waited twelve months. I was, after all, only 19. And then, I was, after all, only 20. Also, I wasn't sure which meeting to belong to. Home? Where I live whilst I'm studying? And finally, almost defiantly, I said, 'It's only a silly letter', and applied in 1995. They nearly didn't visit me, apparently – 'some people don't need visiting'. I'm glad they did. The visit was the highlight of the experience – a feeling of connecting with the two people who came to talk to me, and an opportunity to 'share in those things which are eternal'.

Afterwards, I encountered people who questioned membership, and I explained that for me it was a shorthand – a way of saying, 'yes, I understand the basic precepts of, and I am committed to Quakerism'. Being a member was being part of a community, sharing one voice, sharing a common heritage and common beliefs.

What does unite us as Quakers?
See section **B. Paths and Definitions**.

C4 I feel I belong to the Religious Society of Friends, although I am not a member and do not intend to become a member of my Yearly Meeting in the near future. But my sense of belonging is stronger than the definition of commitment through membership – the question of whether being a member makes me more of a Quaker does not occur to me as I know I am one already.

Do you feel you belong to the Religious Society of Friends? See **C1**.

Does being a member mean you are more committed? **P3**.

C5 I may be only 11, but I am a member. I chose to be a member myself, for a number of reasons. On every Sunday for six or seven years I've gone to Meeting for Worship, and it is a part of my life. Everyone is open and friendly, like a big family that you know you can trust. During the meeting, I feel there is a bond between everyone, a light connecting us together, God or something very strong. That's right for me. I believe there is 'that of God' in every person, that everyone is equal, that anyone can believe what they want, and these and other things helped me decide I wanted to become a Quaker. I have been to meetings of several different Christian denominations as part of a project I did for myself, and found I was most at home with the Quakers. This helped me decide to become a member, and I'm very happy I did, though nothing has really changed. Each person's spiritual life is an amazing and complicated thing for them, and I'm at home with the Quakers so far … there's a lot more to come yet, I hope.

C6   Membership is an optional, but valuable, opportunity for commitment to the Religious Society of Friends. It wasn't until an experimental meeting for worship at YFGM in Oxford that I fully appreciated the impressive aspects of commitment. The structure of the meeting was based around tying a ribbon, if you wished to, around a branch of a small tree. I usually find these activities unhelpful and don't join in or commit myself. However, I received an 'it's your turn now' look and found myself tying my ribbon on the tree, not personally to belong, but to show that person that I was committing myself.

C7   At Yearly Meeting in 1997 I heard this ministry: sitting silently in meeting is a strong commitment to Quakerism, despite people thinking 'well, I won't go to church, but I'll agree to sit in silence – at least it doesn't commit me to anything!'

Isn't one of the great things about silence that it doesn't say anything outwardly about your commitment? Your commitment is allowed to come naturally from the inside, growing to whatever degree is right for the moment.

Could this be the most solid and secure kind of commitment?

Or are we silent because we don't know what to say?

Does silence stop us from understanding our connections? See **E18**.

Is there commitment without action? See **N12**, **N15** *or* **N16**.

C8   I became a member of the Religious Society of Friends just before I left to spend a year overseas, in the knowledge that I was unlikely to find a meeting to attend. At that point the belonging was more important than the commitment; it meant something to me that there would be a place for me to come back to. There was also the wish to be able to call myself a 'Quaker' and mean more than the fact that I happened to be the child of Quaker parents.

Since then, membership has come to mean much more to me. I have gradually tried to take a fuller part in various levels of the operation of the Society. Being a member means never being able to say 'they have decided' or 'they should do this' about any activity which bears the Quaker label, but only 'we'. This feeling is perhaps why my participation in Young Friends General Meeting has been limited, because there are times when YFGM appears to perceive itself as standing against the rest of the Society in Britain.

When I am in a Quaker gathering of any sort, be it my local meeting, Yearly Meeting or a Young Friends event, I've often caught myself recently looking round and thinking about all the people who are not there: nobody in manual work, few from ethnic minorities, no 'Sun' and few 'Telegraph' readers... Commitment and belonging to a group of like-minded people with similar backgrounds is very strengthening and provides a very safe space, but it's vital that such a group doesn't become inward-looking – what is it looking in on, after all? When we, as Quakers, devote our time to talking about what 'we' do, believe, or are, it's worth asking where that leaves everybody who is outside our small and rarefied circle.

I decided recently that I was a Quaker with leanings towards

Anglicanism — not because I have any desire for Anglican ways of worship (except when I feel the need to be theologically challenged rather than coddled), but because I'm attracted to the vision of a church as a spiritual community that seeks to address the needs of a whole society. Belonging to such a church may not necessarily be as conscious a decision, or imply as much, as belonging to the Religious Society of Friends (compare the number of people who label themselves 'C. of E.' with the number who attend church on an average Sunday), but precisely for that reason there is less temptation to draw dividing lines between those who 'belong' and those who do not, and then to concentrate on the needs and concerns of the former group.

Commitment to action... see **N19.**

C9   I belong to the Religious Society of Friends. I have called myself a Quaker all my life and know that it is my spiritual home. When I became a member is immaterial, because I have always been a Quaker.

However, I am not a part of any Meeting for Worship at the moment. I rarely attend meeting. My membership is in a place nowhere near where I live, because of the relationship I have with the meeting in my local area.

I felt I didn't belong right from the start. It has a number of very vocal, dogmatic people. They have read lots and lots of Quaker literature and assume that I have too. They assume that I have the same intellectual curiosity about Quaker writings as they do. They are theologians to me, all words and no substance, and it is because of the dominance of these Friends that I have always felt uncomfortable in the local meeting where I live. I don't belong.

I am an active Friend. I have been very involved with Young Friends Central Committee and Young Friends General Meeting over the last few years. I have been very active centrally in the Society. But I am told by members of the local meeting here that I am doing things wrongly. That word has been used. That it is wrong to belong to the national organisation without belonging primarily to the local meeting. I have been told that I am wrong to say that some people find it easier to belong to the national community than to local meetings. How can I be wrong when it applies at least to me, and to a number of people that I know?

And yet I know I do belong. I know that I don't belong to the meeting geographically nearest to where I live: I don't belong emotionally, spiritually, financially or officially.

YFGM is a community. A year ago, I felt committed to YFGM, I believed in what it tries to do and supported that belief by giving time to help it survive. But I didn't really feel I belonged. I have been attending it for nine years now and have often wondered about wandering off. Then something happens and I don't. Recently it has become clear that it's the spiritual sense of community that I feel at YFGM and don't get in the meeting near where I live that keeps me coming back.

It isn't as simple as the cliché of Young Friends going to YFGM but not to their local meeting. Before I moved to where I am now, I went to my local meeting regularly. I was often at home at weekends and hardly ever missed a Meeting for Worship. I felt a part of that meeting. I feel more a part of a meeting many miles from where I live than I do of the one in my local area.

And yet I remain committed to the Religious Society of Friends. After all I have experienced, I am a Quaker. I know that my spiritual home is within Quakers and I'm happy to be a Quaker. I belong within the Yearly Meeting, but I have come to feel that I don't belong to a Meeting for Worship.

And now I feel that I don't want to belong to my local meeting. I have given up trying. And I am trying to move away from this area in order to be able to belong to a Meeting for Worship. To be a part of a local meeting. To take my gifts to offer to a local meeting and to share as part of a worshipping community the richness of the diversity of a Meeting for Worship. Until then, the community which helps refresh me spiritually, and to which I belong, is YFGM.

Why not belong to both local and national meetings?

The writer of L15 had to search to find a way of belonging.

What could you say to this Friend? Could this be happening in your local Meeting?

C10 What does commitment entail in a faith context? Commitment can be dynamic. Membership of the Religious Society of Friends demands commitment to God, but our understanding and experience of God changes on a daily (hourly?) basis. So where does that leave our commitment?

C11 People often ask me why I am not a member. One answer I used to give flippantly was that if the fascists take power, I want to be working for the aims of the Society outside prison, not inside it! Imagine my horror when an Austrian Catholic acquaintance of mine responded with 'Oh yes, that is very sensible!' She has been involved in non-violent direct action, particularly in connection with the building of roads through environmentally sensitive areas. She is not considered for certain posts in the Roman Catholic Church, because her potential employers have access to files detailing her arrests for taking part in non-violent demonstrations.

Quakers are involved with social and political action,
*see **N. Lifestyle and Responsibility**.*

C12 How much would the UK Government have to change before membership of the Religious Society of Friends would bar me from working as a civil servant? How much would the Society have to change? Has our Society become acceptable in the eyes of the establishment — safe, non-threatening, bland?

C13 I believe that within everybody on earth there is a unique magic. This magic makes everybody divinely special, and as we meet, live with, know and encounter each other, we share this magic and are changed by it. Some people have different names for this magic. To me, what people call it is not important; to me, the thing that is important is that we celebrate it.

Recently, I applied for and was accepted into membership of the Religious Society of Friends. When I was asked at my meeting about what I felt I had to contribute through membership, all I could think to say was 'celebration and joy'.

C14 In meeting last week, a man was welcomed into membership. He stood up, grinned, stretched his arms in the air and cried,
'Yippee!'
An elderly lady across the room murmured,
'How unQuakerly.'
'Oh no!' came the chorus from the meeting, chuckling.

D Young Friends

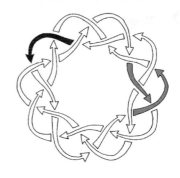

Young Friends

What unites us as Young Friends?

Familiarity with tried and tested methods.	**D9, F10**.
A commitment to attend gatherings, be representatives, work for community.	**D1**.
A current of similarity, despite diversity of lifestyle in group.	**D12**.
Recognition of our community.	**D2**.
Experience of safety.	**D11**.
We are there for each other.	**D8**.
We are welcoming to others and to each other.	**E8**.
Few conditions on acceptance.	**D10**.

D Young Friends

D1 I feel a strong sense of belonging to Quakerism mainly as a result of my involvement with Young Friends activities. I really feel that the atmosphere at Quaker events is one that would be extremely useful within the rest of society as a whole. I always return from Quaker weekends changed, determined to live my whole life, not just my life within Quakerism, in the same open, expressive, 'innocent' way. But repeatedly I find that I become disheartened by the real world and lose that inspiration gradually. I know, however, that since I started being a Young Friend I have changed in so many ways, become much more how I would like to be.

I sometimes wonder what the difference is between being a Young Friend and being the member of an evangelical cult. I think that, although the atmosphere at a basic level may be very similar, with an emphasis on the acceptance of people who quite often don't fit in very well with the people they usually are with, Quakerism holds this acceptance as a 'major premise' rather than using the new-found confidence of formerly isolated people to manipulate them to the particular group's ends. The true ends of Quakerism are the ends of a God we listen to, who is speaking to us all, individually in the silence. I value this very highly indeed.

*More about Young Friends gatherings can be found in **E2**.*

*When acceptance fails: turn to **C9**.*

D2 We validate the spiritual – we act/speak as if there is a divine presence that does make a difference. It's OK to talk spiritually because part of our being together is a belief in that. Many other groups have strong concerns and commitments, but few have outspoken views about the presence of the spiritual within that.

Here, within Young Friends, I stick out less. I feel more normal (what is normal?) – more like the others around me – that I can be me without raised eyebrows or tolerant laughs.

We share our connectedness sometimes: through a shared history of Junior Yearly Meeting, link groups, Senior Conference,

Junior Young Friends groups etc., through involvement with campaigns and concerns, or through our decision to commit ourselves to Quakerism rather than to another society.

Although we don't see each other often there is a sense of shared purpose. Yes, of course, we all have different agendas, we all come for different reasons, we often feel differently about the process and content, but we don't often feel alone in that.

We *do* want to change the world – in different ways, by doing different things – but we believe it important to be doing this.

So what do we do to change the world?
See section **N. Lifestyle and Responsibility**.

D3   Young Friends, unlike other groups with similar concerns, perhaps recognise the presence of a spiritual life, even though many struggle with coming to the validity of the existence of a spiritual life.

D4   As a group we are willing and able to stand by our consciences, to be held up for our beliefs, to change our lives, our living patterns, because of a concern, a strong belief that this needs to be done. To generalise, we have ideals and want to do something to achieve them, and although this doesn't apply specifically and only to Quakerism, it does set us apart from most of the rest of the country's apathetic youth.

Are these our distinguishing features?
Take a look at **E15** *for an expansion on this theme.*

D5   I find Young Friends different from other groups of young people because we seem to be able to 'Be' rather than 'Do', understanding that this is a way of changing the *status* quo, to simply exist (although obviously there is a lot to do as well).

How else are Young Friends 'different'? See **F11**.

For more on 'just being', see **E2**.

D   Young Friends

D6   Just in making Young Friends General Meeting happen, people are affirmed and kept in touch. Of course YFGM *does* do things, but if it didn't, the fact that about 100 people can meet regularly in different cities around Britain would still be good. 'Things happen when Young Friends meet' — it sounds like an advertising slogan!

> *YFGM does not meet all that often — only three times a year — does it matter?*

D7   I am not really committed to Young Friends General Meeting — yet I reap the spiritual benefits of being involved in an organisation that challenges and expands my assumptions and beliefs. I don't make YFGM a priority in my life because my other commitments come first. I feel I belong, without making a commitment. Arrogant attitude of mine. It must be a very special organisation where this is possible.

What hinders my commitment? All the time needed for self-maintenance, such as nominations etc. Pettiness. YFGM is stressful. So much to do, too little time, don't get to talk to friends properly.

What encourages it? People — friends. Enjoyment. Feeling involved, that I belong. Passion for the issues.

> *The time needed for maintaining the structure itself is perceived as a problem in the Society: see* **F17**.

D8   There is a passion among Young Friends, a need to go out into the world and make things better. I feel this need strongly, and it is wonderful to be among Young Friends and feel that this need is shared, that others understand where I am coming from. Others may have different ways of expressing and acting on this, but it is understood by all.

> *See* **P5**.

D9   What unites Young Friends? Common beliefs within a diverse group. Within the group of Young Friends there is a huge diversity of lifestyle, experience, relationships. This is very exciting and liberating – when we meet I can talk to people about things they are doing, adventures, travels, work, new experiences.

But what makes Young Friends so special and unique for me is that within this web of diversity runs a thread of common experience. Certain things that I hold very dear, such as silent worship, the Quaker business method etc. are accepted: I don't have to explain them or justify them or defend them while I'm here – they just are.

Acceptance of yourself and acceptance of others – made easier when it seems as if everyone is trying to see the best in everyone else. I like hearing people talking about others with such warmth and love.

Diversity – as mentioned in **D12**.

Acceptance and love are linked again here – this seems to be a common concept in discussions about Quakers in general as well – see **E6**.

D10   Young Friends are united by a sense of the divine that accepts a range of differing views. We are united by wanting tolerance, honesty and peace, by what we commonly call 'the testimonies' and by our shared structures and language. These bring us together and give us our sense of belonging.

We can have fun without being flippant, be serious without being sombre.

Working towards fulfilling/living our testimonies is our commitment – how well we achieve this isn't as important as the fact that we try. I wish I had the strength to try harder.

Contrast with **E6**.

So what are we actually doing?
Read **N. Lifestyle and Responsibility**.

D   Young Friends

D11   There is a sense of unity within Young Friends that comes from a respect for each other's beliefs and actions. Our aim is not to judge people; we try to value them for being themselves.

D12   Are we united as Young Friends particularly by our youth? No. We are all at completely different stages – youth does not necessarily imply a common experience.

D13   We might not be physically or chronologically 'young', but Young Friends share a kind of 'young-ness'. At Young Friends General Meeting, I feel that we're all working towards some good together, even though we might feel isolated and purely self-sustaining at home. I feel a more spiritual bond with friends I know through Young Friends, as if they have a 'spiritual' dimension to them. It appears in ethics, shopping, work, social action etc.

D14   What unites us as Young Friends? There's a short answer: God! There's a creative spark, an energy that flows between us in our gatherings. We feel warm and welcomed and inspired. God is there in other groups too, but some things make us particularly open to the Spirit with other Young Friends.

*See **E8** for a similar thought.*

*What makes us feel warm and welcome? Look at **E2**.*

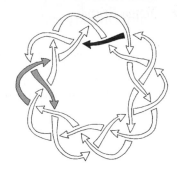

Unity, Diversity & Acceptance

What unites us as Quakers?

Shared ideals. Try **E6**.

We are willing to validate others even when
we arc not in agreement. Try **E18**.

We are united as Quakers by the fact that we are
constantly striving to look for goodness in everyone. *See* **E16**.

Shared history, Quaker business meetings, knowledge of jargon,
silence – those outward forms are important too because they are
familiar and because they engender a sense of belonging for me.

F9 looks critically at the business method.

Have you ever experienced an 'awkward silence' among Friends?

E   Unity, Diversity and Acceptance

E1   Because Young Friends meet much less often than a preparative meeting, and a different combination of people attends each time, Young Friends General Meeting is a strange thing to belong to. There is an ongoing feeling of unity, however. There is an acceptance that others here are also trying to express what is in their hearts.

Do we share a sense of belonging together although we do not meet frequently?

E2   For me, Young Friends gatherings provide an opportunity to be relaxed and open in an environment in which I know I will not be criticised for the views and beliefs that I have. The sense of unity we feel comes from the belief that every one of us is important and equal and has a valid contribution to make. It is the ability to see 'that of God' in everyone that unites us so closely.

In my day-to-day life it is difficult to be open and true about who I am and what I believe, due to the fact that those around me are not as open and accepting as I need them to be.

Do we have the same opportunity to be 'relaxed and open' at other Quaker gatherings? Is this an objective or something that comes automatically?

*Can we bring this openness into everyday life? Look at **D1**.*

E3   One and a half years ago I moved to a village in a rural area and attended the Quaker meeting there. I found the members of the meeting to be kind, generous and friendly. I felt like the odd-one-out to start with, because I was the youngest in meeting by about 30 years, but I was sure that this would pass as I got to know the other Friends. I attended the meeting almost every Sunday that I could, but I was often away on training courses or on Young Friends General Meeting business. I wanted to belong to the meeting in my village. However, each time I finally got a free Sunday and could go to meeting, I was singled out by the clerk and welcomed back as if I were a rare visitor. How kind! – but after a year I still felt excluded. They made it clear that I was still the odd-one-out.

Are we too sensitive or too insensitive? Whose responsibility is it to make an individual belong to a group?

Who decides if you belong? See **L6**.

The writer of **C9** *had a different excluding experience.*

E4   Although everything may be going brilliantly in my life, it is only through Quakers and meeting that I will really stop and reflect. This is easy to do because of the supportive and unquestioning atmosphere that tends to surround most Quaker and Young Friends events. The feeling of being accepted creates a sense of belonging to the group.

E5   Young Friends are not a 'common interest' group. Our uniting ties are not what we do but who we are.

Are we tolerant, spiritual, honest people? What do you think it is about who we are that unites us?

E6   We show commitment to Young Friends General Meeting by carrying some sense of shared values over into the rest of our lives. Both within YFGM and outside it we try to be accepting, caring and loving towards other people – following the 'promptings of love and truth'.

E7   I often think that to people who I encounter in my day-to-day life I may not appear committed to Quakerism at all: I rarely go to meeting, but I do try to live by my spiritual beliefs and I certainly feel a strong sense of belonging to Quakerism. I often think how great it is to be able to go to any meeting, anywhere, and be welcomed and feel accepted and not have to justify my beliefs. This feeling of acceptance seems to me one of the most important things about Quakerism.

See **N15** *for a way of living worshipfully.*

E Unity, Diversity and Acceptance

E8 United by God? It's a wonderful idea, and if I stop and think about it for a while, then I find I like it, although it isn't mine and that isn't language I would normally use. For me, God is what we make of it, and I find that the sense of connectedness is strongest in meetings with Young Friends.

Can you be committed without action? What does commitment mean if you don't feel you really belong, or if you feel there is no sense of belonging? I find this a hard question in relation to Young Friends General Meeting, as some feel we are a real unit, but I have to disagree. The constant flux of membership means that groupings of past acquaintances always change, and there is never a chance for less outgoing people to get to know everyone.

E9 Although we may come from different backgrounds, we have many things in common: caring about other people, a social conscience, some degree of pacifism, tolerance… These things that we have in common make it possible for us to relax and open up to each other, so that the Spirit flows freely. We can raise energy as a group and trust that it will be used wisely. Having this energy focused on you is an amazing feeling – for example, when the clerks are writing a difficult minute and the meeting upholds them; as clerk I have experienced really strong support.

*Try **D9** for more on the 'web of common experience' within YFGM.*

E10 Belonging happens in a nebulous, unco-ordinated way. In being accepted by others, we belong. In committing ourselves, we belong.

E11 Commitment and belonging are closely linked concepts and can induce both positive and negative feelings. Belonging to a group can provide support and confidence. However, it can encourage pride, possessiveness and dependence, and a hostility to change or to outsiders.

Commitment often arises out of a sense of belonging (for example, marriage or membership), although it may be through sustained commitment to any particular club or cause that we come to belong to it. Commitment can be a burden or a prison. However, it can provide a focus for action and create a sense of security.

E12 Belonging (as far as I know it) is the exact opposite of feeling threatened – it is a link that gives security and comfort. Belonging in a place is when it feels like home. Belonging in a group of people is when you feel they want you: you can be yourself and feel loved. Perhaps the difference between simply being accepted in a place and belonging there is the difference between being liked and being loved. I am often accepted, but I do not often realise it, and I rarely feel I belong. I've found that, linked to a lack of commitment, whether as a cause or an effect I don't know, maybe both, is a lack of security and belonging. There have been very few times and places in my life in which I've felt I belong and fit in, and felt comfortable. With both belonging and commitment, there are always different degrees of involvement, of how far in you are, but I haven't felt comfortable enough to stop in any situation for very long, and never comfortable enough to stop completely.

E13 Why am I a Quaker?
I find it strange that people come to Quakerism who say that they are atheists, who feel uncomfortable with Christian language. How can you be a Quaker without recognising those promptings to love and truth? Quakerism is designed for dealing with those promptings. A lot of Young Friends say they don't believe in God. This is where language and labels hinder us. Our impulses are the same, and I believe they derive from the same force. I reject, however, any 'Quakerism' that does not focus to some extent on spirituality. A non-spiritual Quaker is an anomaly.
Yet...
I am not always sensible of this force in myself and sometimes I find it hard to sense it in others. I have spiritual dry patches, when my commitment to the organisation of the Religious Society of Friends

wanes and I wonder if I am all talk and no action. It is then that I question the mechanisms we have in place for exploring spirituality (and as an intrinsic part of that, the way we act on those spiritual impulses) – because I wonder if everyone else is all talk and no action. And for those who are no thought and all action, who don't even believe in spirituality, just in the values and culture of Friends, how can our processes be the correct ones?

E14 To me it is important that the Religious Society of Friends is not labelled a Christian group. I find one of the most exciting things about the Society is that it changes, it reinterprets itself, it reflects the direct experience of its members. Christians have creeds, and to me that implies a caging of the spirit, a boxing in, an attempt to define something that is too big to be described in words. We can take snapshots but they are only from one angle at one moment in time.

Sadly, many people merely wander into the Society as disenchanted Christians who want to acknowledge the spiritual side of life but ignore the baggage of holy wars, Christian dogma, inquisitions and the church. This can suppress doubts and deep questioning.

As to the split between Christian and universalist, in Meeting for Worship it seems to me that the differences subside and I can find that of God in the statements of anyone who ministers. I think this points to the existence of many ways to the truth and the validity of everyone's truth. I don't think there is a problem as long as people feel they still belong and are accepted.

If we advertise ourselves as Christian, then I think a lot of potential enquirers who would have found their home in the Society would be put off.

E15 I used to think that anyone who did not believe in God was out of place in the Religious Society of Friends. It is a *religious* Society, after all. We can cope with Christocentrics and universalists, but atheists?

Then I started talking to a particularly insightful person I know from Young Friends General Meeting. He turns out to be rather on the atheist side of agnostic. Yet he finds YFGM a great place to come to develop his spirituality and to find people to work together with for peace, equality, truth and simplicity. How could I not want my friend to be part of the Society? I was prodded into examining why I wanted only believers in God to be Quakers.

I discovered that I was afraid that in a group of atheists it would be difficult for me to talk about God. I was afraid that with atheists in business meetings we would be unable to produce statements and write letters mentioning God. It is only with Quakers that I feel able to talk about God without being laughed at or causing offence, and this is really precious to me.

I compared my position as a universalist worrying about atheists to the position of a Quaker Christian worrying about universalists. There are a lot of similarities between the two positions. Quakers in the past have largely been strongly Christian; the Christocentrics must have the same fear that their heritage might be stolen from them, that their right to talk about Jesus, the Son of God, might be lost if the general attitude in their meetings changes.

As a universalist I want to say to them, 'Don't worry! I don't share your belief in the extraordinary deity of Jesus, but I still think he was an amazing person and well worth mentioning. If you suggest a good minute with Jesus' name in it, I shall be happy to accept it, either thinking that it is another name for God or thinking of what an amazing person He was.'

I am confident that a Quaker Christocentric's belief in Jesus is very unlikely to lead them to any action I feel uncomfortable with, and I want to join with them in learning about God and putting our faith into action. We can surely achieve more by working together.

Suppose three of us suddenly jump up in meeting. The first person says, 'Jesus is telling me to do something about homelessness.' I say, 'God is telling me to do something about homelessness.' My friend says, 'My conscience is telling me to do something about homelessness.' I may think to myself, 'Ha! He hasn't realised yet that that's God talking!' and he may think to himself 'She's kidding herself about God, that's her conscience talking!' – but that won't stop us from going out and doing something about homelessness together!

> *Is what we are experiencing the same, while we perceive*
> *it in different ideas and use different language about it*
> *because we have different associations?*

E16 I've been asking myself quite frequently recently whether I belong in the Religious Society of Friends. I've just applied for membership so I guess this suggests that I feel I do belong in the Society. Naturally, there are some things about the Society which I'm really fond of, some which I'm totally committed to (or aim to be), some things which I don't have that sense of belonging to, and some which I'm absolutely uncommitted to (in fact, I'm committed to challenging them). I don't see this as a bad thing at all though – quite the opposite. It's the diversity of the Society that I love: the fact that people with a whole variety of beliefs can come together and at the same time seem to have something that unites us. What is it that unites us then? Does something unite us?

I think that the one way to work out what does unite us is to ask what divides us from the rest of society. Sure, you could say that the Religious Society of Friends is made up totally of humans (well, I think so), but this doesn't make us any different from Jo Public. I've heard that there has been some debate recently about a member of Sinn Fein who was refused membership of the Society – that it was their support of an organisation that condoned violence that prompted their monthly meeting to refuse them membership. I'm sure that there are other things that would prevent people entering the Society – a denial that there is 'that of God in everyone', for instance.

I'll get to the point. What I reckon unites us is a belief in the testimonies. I don't believe that everyone is totally committed to the same degree, but it seems everyone believes that we *ought* to seek 'that of God in everyone', that we *ought* not to be violent whatever the end, that we ought to be honest. What I don't reckon unites us any more is any sort of specific labelling of our 'spirituality'. There seem to be representatives of all sorts of beliefs in the Society – atheists, agnostics, Buddhists, Christians, humanists, pagans, spiritualists, universalists. Do you think that someone who is a really fab person – really honest, peace-loving, with a respect for all – should be denied membership if they don't put a spiritual label on their belief that there is something good in everyone?

I really don't care what the identity of my spirituality is, if you can call it spirituality. All that I'm interested in is how I live it out and how it is nurtured. In the same way, I'm not interested in what the Society's spiritual basis is. As long as we acknowledge that there is 'that of God in everyone', that everyone has the potential to be good, I'm not bothered what we believe. What I am bothered about is how our beliefs are translated into action. If you help those in need, I don't care if your motivation is God or a desire to do good. How can you be committed to something if it doesn't show in your actions?

If the Religious Society of Friends corporately believes that there is 'that of God in everyone', why don't we let everyone into the Society? Because there are things that we believe we ought to be committed to – the testimonies. Quite simply, we can only commit ourselves as a Society to what we are united behind. Our diversity is due to the variety of ways in which we belong. Can't we recognise that we're no longer united by a spiritual theme? Aren't we united by the testimonies?

Are what are commonly called 'the testimonies' a common fruit of our ultimately inexpressible root beliefs? See **B7**.

Testimonies unite us… see **P6**.

E17 At the 1995 Manchester conference, I heard conflicting views: 'God is constructed by humanity'; 'God is a presence, exterior to humanity'; 'We should dig deep in our heritage, and only our heritage'; 'We should listen to diversity'.

E   Unity, Diversity and Acceptance

I wondered whether Quakers could really be part of the same community and differ on these things. A Young Friend ministered at the end of a session, 'We don't share beliefs. We share values.' An older Friend ministered, 'Yes, but there has to be a limit to our diversity of belief. A circumference within which we all share something'. In spite of apparently conflicting messages, I felt sure there was a unity, elusive because of our personal histories and our language barriers. We were all guided by something spiritual.

Is it true that 'you don't have to be a Christian but you'd better be a pacifist'? See **P5**.

E18 It is easy in this kind of group to feel safe and understood – perhaps it is too easy. Perhaps to a certain extent we have stopped trying to communicate what we mean by spirituality, what our real experiences are, what we feel in relation to each other. We are all different, and unless we are willing to share and explore our differences we will never really understand our unity.

I have a commitment to doubt, to putting effort into my best ability, trying to recognise truth and respond to it.

> *The writer of* **F9** *has doubts, but*
> *ultimately continues to be a Quaker.*

I'm not sure 'committed' is the word. I have an *awareness*. I haven't made a commitment, though I hope my awareness of my windspirit becomes clearer as I live more of my life and have more experience. My commitment to this general goal prompts me to try to make space in my life for prayer and meditation and thinking about the Goddess/God, and leads me to be interested in discussing spirituality, sometimes obscurely through many distractions.

> *Is your spiritual commitment to yourself or to an organisation?*
> **F5** *looks at commitment to a process.*

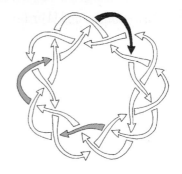

Discernment and Worship

How committed are you to worship?

I'm committed, I think, to going to meeting and to other events with silent togetherness so that I can find this godly way and help others find it.

F6 questions this 'godly way' during Meeting for Worship.

I'm committed to this path through my attitude to the world and to other people, through the work that I do, through the things that I think about and the actions I take.

N2 examines this attitude.

I'm trying to use Meeting for Worship in a spiritually responsible way: to read (more); to be open to others' articulations of spirituality; to attempt to create opportunities to be close to God, for example, by meditating on an idea, being in a beautiful or challenging place, listening to people and being more open to the Bible.

Preparation for Meeting for Worship can be helpful in this way... F13.

F   Discernment and Worship

F1   I find that spiritual communion has to happen with the whole of me, and I think Quakers have always had this – the fire, the quaking, the uplifted feelings are all very physical. I find that the path of systematically denying the body is unloving, and it is my experience that bodily 'visions' and the truest feelings of wholeness come with a careful listening to my centre where my parts are joined. I feel that the inspiring fire in my belly is the place where my soul joins my body. It is from here that my deepest inspirations arise, in Meeting for Worship, in meditation, in those random moments of wonder, while travelling, sitting, thinking. My soul reaches out higher, wider than my body can see and down through the ground that I walk on. It is an antenna, a channel. It catches insights, overlaps with others' souls and relays messages from the universe, from godde.

B1 *contains another experience of the 'powerful force'.*

F2   I walk through one of the parks. It is summer. There is a huge avenue of trees, rich, green, wind-rustled. I feel my dress move against my legs in the heat. I am upset; I am scared. In the peace of the trees, the stately grandeur of the avenue, I feel comforted. I am held.

I am in Meeting for Worship. My emotions simmer, my calm ruffled, fury absorbing me. I wonder if I can bear the stillness for another 30 minutes and consider slipping out and going for a walk. Then the silence takes over. A piece of ministry clicks with my experience, and a phrase of a well-known poem moulds two ideas together. My heart starts thumping and I tell it to stop. It keeps beating – adrenaline rush. I speak. My voice sounds strange, too fast, too quiet; my words are badly ordered. I can't stop the ministry.

I am at my desk; it is very late. I have just finished writing my Swarthmore Lecture contribution. I think about my interview next week. I wonder how convinced I am about the career I am considering. I think about faith and action. I know strongly that that career is not for me, not yet. I put some music on, voices and oboe, pulling my emotions along with it. I feel convinced, passionate, moved.

F3 Our commitment as Quakers to seeking the will of godde is about the most important commitment I have in my life. I'm not saying I manage to do it all the time, but when I remember it I do, and I'm getting better at remembering! The idea of questioning even how I'm thinking about things is something I have to do, pulling my life into a coherent whole by leaning on the string that leads to godde. The other traditions we have as Quakers – the things like honesty, integrity and non-violence – spring naturally from the awareness of godde's will.

The Friend who wrote **F11** *is also committed to questioning.*

F4 To talk of peace in our times cannot be done lightly. The tragic lack of peace around the world is linked with the lack of commitment to understanding what it means to create it within our lives and societies. As a 'peace church', the responsibility of Friends to the work of peace is considerable. It demands radical change in our lives and in the way we relate to each other, to the world outside, to the Spirit, to ourselves. As Friends we have a heritage of experience and testimonies to ways of finding peace and living peace. Our task today is to test our Quaker methods and processes, to listen to what the Spirit is requiring of us now and to answer the question which has sounded through the centuries, 'What canst thou say?'.

What canst thou say? **N13** *gives a personal answer.*

F5 How do we square commitment with flexibility and an open mind?
My primary commitment is not to a body or organisation, but to a *process* (of searching), which requires flexibility. Honesty and confidence about your commitments can *enable* and *require* flexibility and an open mind: you can approach other ideas with honesty and confidence if you have your own framework to relate them to. If you have no framework, you may become reactive and fearful of alternative ideas as you blow with the wind. This implies a radical challenge

– of commitment to ideas and processes you are prepared ultimately to abandon – and the realisation that, as everything has its mystery, you will never *totally* understand. Quakerism tries to square this dilemma with a non-doctrinal approach.

Should this mystery remain undefined? See **B7** *for one approach.*

Love being behind our commitments... **P8**.

F6   Do we really find God in Meeting for Worship? People talk of meeting 'refuelling their energies', being a 'space for themselves in the week'. They talk of 'clearing their minds', 'centring down'. Is this really being open to the promptings of the Spirit? How can we know if everyone is experiencing the same thing? Meeting for Worship unites me to the rest of the Religious Society of Friends, because our contemplative worship marks us as Quakers, as much as our commitment to the promptings of the Spirit. Sometimes I doubt my commitment to that hour of contemplation, worship and prayer, and so I doubt others' commitment to it too.

In Meeting for Worship, my mind fidgets. I think about my relationships with people, and mock conversations and letters filter through my head. I try to focus on something, maybe that I've read that week, and stray off immediately to my work or to an encounter I had the other day. I look at all these people in silence and think what others might think of our strange practices. I become aware of myself sitting in the same position every week, unfocused every week, too absorbed by my thoughts and by how this experience is no different to sitting on a park bench on my own.

And then, sometimes, I become 'awe-full' of what we do. I become aware of the intensity of 30 or 70 or 1000 people gathered together in silence. Sometimes I pray – I focus on one person in my thoughts, and hold them in my light, loving them from the centre of my heart. At other times I catch a glimpse of the glistening stillness amongst us. Sometimes I am moved by the truth of a piece of ministry, or challenged by it, and my mind races or reposes. Once or twice I have been dragged from complete disinvolvement, from sentiments of anger and frustration, when I have been about to leave the meeting because I am so outside of its contemplative stillness, to an experience of the Divine which takes me by surprise. Meeting for Worship happens to me.

I firmly believe that Meeting for Worship can be at the heart of my Quakerism. It is certainly the community which gives me the space for my spiritual journeying, and for me is the 'home' to which I would like to belong. I find my belonging and commitment to it problematic, but I know that it will sometimes be a necessary part of discerning the promptings of the Spirit.

The 'idea' of Quakerism is part of me. I seek to take heed of the promptings of love and truth. I want to have the intention, called 'Love', of being open to the Spirit. I feel that the dance of action is part of the stillness of my belief.

Could you do anything about the way your mind wanders,
if you wanted to? See **F13**.

Other experience of Meeting for Worship… see **B1**.

Quakerism as a community… **C9**.

F7 In my local meeting there is a lack of openness to change and new ideas and also a slackness in upholding the business method. I feel a lack of acceptance of me as an individual. I don't feel I belong there and rarely go. I have tried to resolve my commitments to my local meeting and make it clear I don't wish to fake anymore. At Young Friends (General Meeting) I know I can be myself even when that's not nice. It means I can continue my historic roots in the Religious Society of Friends without the prejudice of small-minded individuals.

Do you want to read more criticism of our use of the business method, that
we all, at least in theory, have in common? Turn to **F17**.

What's so special about YFGM, then? See **D2**.

F8   I go to Meeting for Worship to think, to have space, to sort through my feelings. I find it beneficial; I notice when I've not been in Meeting for Worship for a while. I lived at Woodbrooke for a term, and going to meeting every morning was a very important part of being there. My thoughts are likely to turn to friends and lovers, to my feelings and emotions for these people in my life. I may replay a conversation, contemplating the words, and more, that we shared. I may look ahead, think about what I want to do in the next day or two, people I would like to contact, feelings and thoughts I'd like to share. Sometimes I dream of what I'd like to happen, the way I'd like my life to be, and of how those dreams could be reality, NOW.

I rarely think about godde, about my spiritual life, and this rarely worries me. I would like to be more aware of the workings of my godde in my life, but also I strongly trust my inner instinct, my intuition, and, to some extent, believe that is how my godde is working. I am sometimes aware of my godde, of her strength, her power. It always seems to be a positive force: I feel that she is smiling with me and that she too is enjoying my life. I am committed to living a life which I feel is 'right' in my work, my relations with others, my way of living, and I feel that this is following the will of my godde. I believe that, although I have little awareness of this, my life is guided.

This is probably another way of saying that I believe that the whole of life is sacramental. Either nothing is spiritual, or everything is, and as I have been aware of a greater presence than just me, I suspect that everything is spiritual. I suspect that, although I don't think deliberately of my spirituality, of my godde, I am, in fact, doing this all the time: all my actions, thoughts, etc., are coming from a deep spiritual motivation.

> *Although Quakers all do, in theory at least, believe there is no division between the sacred and the secular, do we really manage to live our lives this way? See* **N11** *for thoughts on this idea.*

F9   I had doubts. If no one else believed in something spiritual, could I be sure that what I believed in was something spiritual? And if we did not share the divine impulse to action, then what the hell was going on in our business method? How did we know that the decisions we were taking were divinely led? The business method seemed to me to be the fundamental expression of what we did: true belief in action. If that failed, perhaps Quakers were failing.

My first experience of preparative meeting is a case in point, even if the subject sounds fairly trivial. I was twelve at the time. PM was trying to decide whether the children should go into meeting for the first or the last fifteen minutes. The 11+ children's group felt so strongly that the current format of going in for the first 15 minutes should be retained that we turned up in force to state our case. We got labelled the 'backbenchers'. We didn't want our in-depth discussions in children's class curtailed. We thought it would disrupt the worship to have over forty children coming into meeting, tramping in, looking for their parents, giggling... Coming into a gathered meeting? We'd never experienced a gathered meeting anyway. Our wishes were upheld.

With the benefit of hindsight, I see that that opinion was wrong. In Edinburgh and Bakewell meetings, before the notices, the children tell the adults what they've been doing, and vice versa, and then the children hear the visitors introduce themselves, hear the notices, hear the concerns of the meeting reflected in the dates for the diary. Everyone knows what is going on in their community.

So what led us to speak up? Stubbornness? A sense of group purpose? The thrill of being listened to? I don't think it was God. But I do think the meeting was right to give our views weight, in spite of our youth. However, the experience proves to me that our theocratic business method can be hijacked by weightiness, egos and stubbornness, and that you can think you are indisputably right even when you may not be. Our business method is open to abuse if people don't listen to each other and to the Spirit.

I wondered how to ensure that people listened to the Spirit, and in the process began to question whether we were all doing the same thing when applying the business method. A video from Woodbrooke outlined two conflicting ideas whilst presenting them as harmoniously coexisting:

1. In Quaker business meetings, we uncover the will of God: the final solution is the only thing that God wants us to do.
2. In Quaker business meetings, we can reach any number of decisions but the process we use is divine.

The two seemed to me to be mutually exclusive, unable to coexist if our business method was to be viable. How could I be committed to a 'divinely led' group of people who didn't know what 'the divine' was, or how they were to be led? How hypocritical! How hollow! All theory and no practice. All talk and no substance.

The business meetings I went to became more frustrating. Quakers seemed reluctant to define the divine and say, even personally, how it worked for them, so I couldn't be sure there was any 'will of God' in the business meetings. But also, the emphasis on each person's voice being valid meant that we were all a bunch of well-meaning amateurs without the appropriate knowledge to make informed decisions.

Agenda. Membership. One retraction. Application for dual membership – Religious Society of Friends and Catholicism. How does she reconcile the ritual of Catholicism and the simplicity of Quakerism? How does she handle the hierarchy of Catholicism? Does she really believe that the only way to God is through Christ? That women aren't valid preachers? Oh. Tolerance. Acceptance. Ecumenism. Meeting house roof repairs. I'm not an architect. Asylum seekers with no shelter. That's terrible. I wish I could help. But I have no space or money. And I'm not a benefits expert. Nuclear Proliferation Treaty. I don't know anything. Is this really the best way to witness for peace? Employment of wardens. Are we managing them well enough? Or are we being too nice and lacking clarity? I know nothing about employment law, management techniques… I'm not an expert. I don't know enough. I'm only me, looking for God, not sure who God is and what God thinks we should do.

Answer? Trust. 'Trust the process', I'd tell myself grudgingly when my suggestion was not adopted. 'Trust the nominations committee', as I got accepted onto a committee on which I discovered I duplicated experience and could add little to the discussion because of my lack of expertise. 'Trust him/her. They seem to know what they're talking about', as we agreed to a new roof/a change of wardens/a Catholic-Quaker. But I know from student politics that one speech can entirely sway the whole meeting, and then another can sway us all back again. It depends on what you know and how you say it. And why wasn't I telling myself, 'Trust God'?

I have lost confidence. I distrust our basis of faith, and I distrust the effectiveness of our processes. They take up so much time. Time gets vacuumed up for Quakers – weekends away; representatives to this council, that gathering; planning committees; local, regional, national business; international business. I kept thinking, 'I can't criticise without offering a solution'. I wrote half a story all about 'The Quaker Business Monster'. She was fed with time, energy and inspiration, and she had become incredibly fat, because all her energy was wasted trying to convey messages from her brain to her limbs. She couldn't move very far. But I couldn't work out how she got thinner. Similarly, I couldn't work out how the business process could improve. Delegation? More trust? A report in The Friend in February 1997 described the terrible feelings of Friends House staff after a restructuring process which seemed to expose a flawed business method, and joked that all representatives on Meeting for Sufferings should have a National Vocational Qualification in management. I decided the joke was too good to be funny. What an excellent idea! Too many well-meaning amateurs spoil the broth.

So. Do I stay and change from within, or do I get out?

I wouldn't leave. I am a Quaker, whether I am a member of the Religious Society of Friends or not. The culture is ingrained. Membership itself isn't essential to the business process, but the process of making a commitment to Quakerism, to action intertwined with faith, to the principle that one should heed the promptings of truth and love, is essential. The membership process is a good enough one to undergo in an approach to commitment. I just want us to be a bit clearer about what we are committing ourselves to.

More to the point, I believe in God. And I believe in faith intertwined with action. I guess, ultimately, that I trust we will struggle on with our business method and our processes, and occasionally hear that still small voice.

Does it matter whether in our business meetings we are seeking the will of God or seeking in a divine way? See **F15** *for another angle on the question. Does it work, in either case?*

To read more about membership, turn to **C1, C8,** *or any other contribution in section* **C. Membership.**

F10   I feel I belong to Young Friends General Meeting because I don't have to explain why I'm going and why I enjoy it. We are united by a common process, not just by the Quaker business method, but by the way the whole organisation works. It's a process because we are sustained by something ongoing, which is the way our faith is translated into action. The underlying faith or spirituality is what the process is built on and constructed of, and the way we live out our faith is its mechanism.

This is an experience which you cannot understand fully until you have had it. This is like seeing a colour: you can understand the physics of experiencing red, its wavelength, the physiology of the retina when light from a red object falls on it – but you don't know what red is until you've experienced it. If you're colour-blind, you can know all these facts but never have the experience.

But this means the Quaker process is accessible to all who are open to it. It doesn't require you to know facts, just to have the experience. It can't really be fully explained, but everyone who has experienced it knows what I mean. It's why we all feel we belong, and it's what unites us.

Try **D4** *or* **E9** *for why we belong to YFGM.*

Is this what the author of **D11** *was writing about?*

F11 Young Friends General Meeting is a radical, religious, reflective organisation. We hope we are revolutionary. We try to live up to ideas of mutual respect. We have a commitment to the truth of our experience.

This means I question the 'why' of things – why do we apply the Quaker business method in this way? It means we get a better understanding of the way it works, because we question its necessity, as many older Friends (I feel) do not.

So what are we actually doing?
See **N. Lifestyle and Responsibility**.

F12 In Young Friends General Meeting, a sense of belonging comes from being part of a community A warm, spiritual, worshipping community. I don't know what I worship, I don't know what other Friends at YFGM worship. I guess we probably all worship the same kinds of things, only with different words. Nature, Spirit, God, Allah, Creator: it doesn't really matter what it's called,

F13 Preparation before Meeting for Worship enables me to get more out of it. Walking to meeting – a good half hour – does two things: it relaxes my body so I can sit still for an hour, and clears my head of the thoughts of the week I haven't yet processed so I can really listen instead of think.

What do you do in Meeting for Worship? **F8** *tells one story.*

F14   On the last night of a week-long residential work-camp, we gathered round the bonfire to make music and talk over the events of the week. Giovanni and I were two of the last to arrive. The ground was very wet, so we looked for spaces on the logs that had been rolled close to the fire. There was no space on the logs, but we found two cut-off stumps and rolled them up to the only space in the circle of firelight. However, we were soon coughing and weeping from the smoke. We moved back and perched behind the ring of volunteers on their logs. It was cold outside the circle and we could not hear what was being said. We could not see the fire, just the backs of the people in front of us. I waited for someone to roll the logs back to widen the circle and make space for us. After all, we had been working and living together for a week and had been getting on pretty well together – wouldn't our friends welcome us into the circle?

After a while I started to think that the people round the bonfire hadn't noticed us. I tapped the chap in front of me on the shoulder. 'Excuse me, I wonder if you could move up a little bit and make space for me and Giovanni? It's rather cold back here away from the fire.' To my amazement he replied 'No, we're OK'. I asked him again but he did not want to move from his comfortable position. I could hardly believe it. I still cannot understand why someone I had enjoyed working with could leave me out in the cold. Did he not understand how hurt I felt, or did he not care? In the end I stomped off to find somewhere to cry in private.

There are all sorts of ways in which people may unwittingly make someone feel excluded from a group, but surely physical exclusion is so obvious as to be downright rude?

Ever since, I have felt very sensitive to the effects of the physical arrangement of people in groups. If a speaker faces rows of chairs, it is very easy for the people in the rows to doze off or to heckle in their illusion of anonymity. If the same number of people are arranged in a circle with the speaker in the same sort of chair as the audience, the effect is much more intimate. Everyone is included in the event.

In my experience of many Quaker meetings, the clerk, elders

and 'weighty friends' often sit in the more prominent positions, leaving shy people and newcomers to sit in the rows at the back. This makes me feel profoundly uncomfortable. There may indeed be a whole spectrum of involvement in a Quaker meeting, but this is surely irrelevant in a Meeting for Worship? I feel that we are failing to welcome shy people properly by not inviting them to join our circle. In most meetings I have seen, it would easily be possible to accommodate the largest number of worshippers who usually attend in one or two circles in the room.

[I think that] the circle (or concentric circles) is the most appropriate layout for a business meeting, for the following reason. If the members of the meeting are sitting in rows facing the clerk or clerks, they cannot see everyone in the meeting and will tend to address the table rather than the meeting. Since the clerk is there to record the decisions of the meeting and not to take part in making them, this puts them in an uncomfortable position.

F15 One of the problems I see with the Quaker business method is that people say, 'it's not just consensus decision-making – it's seeking the will of God'. When someone uses the G-word most people, I think, unconsciously start thinking 'out there' – that the voice of the transcendent Deity/Spirit will somehow boom from the ether as if from the megaphone of the cosmic riot-squad.

As I see the will of godde, it is consensus decision-making – of a sort. An immanent view of creation – 'Christ has come to teach his people himself' – leads me to the realisation that people are, in their inmost selves, loving, creative, co-operative, divine. The Goddess is manifest in us, as part of creation. I see the face of godde as my anointed self – the inward Christ. The 'consensus', then, that we should reach is that of our essential divine, shared nature.

When I'm trying to discern a course of action for myself, I even use a sort of 'lonesome' Quaker business method. I'll describe to myself, maybe even write down, what the situation is. Then I'll sit and listen around it for a sense of rightness of action, making sure I'm listening to all the parts of me – body self, young self etc. And then I'll find some words to sum it up so I don't forget. I may be idealising it, but the way we conduct our meetings for church affairs expresses to me our commitment to synthesis, to seeking the will of godde in all that we do, not just for an hour on Sundays or when we are with other Quakers.

It helps me, when centring down for worship or unsure of the will of godde in a business meeting, to chant to myself (sub-vocally), 'godde is here because I am here'. I visualise taking off my 'crust', my skin, hardened by the poison in the world of cities and hatred. I experience a feeling, getting my true worth fixed in me, of being a 'shining one' – a Child of Light.

Then I move my attention to someone else in the room who I know and love well, and chant at them, 'godde is here because you are here, godde is in you', until I can see/feel the divinity radiating out of them as well. Next I choose someone I don't know too well and pull the immanent Spirit-Seed into my consciousness of them, and so on. When I have done that I mentally encompass the whole group in a glowing field, letting myself see the tongues of flame around our heads, and I chant to myself 'godde is here, godde is here, we are here' until I'm settled to a level of consciousness I can maintain until the group breaks up.

When we are having difficulty with a decision, getting in the way of ourselves, I might be saying to myself 'godde, godde, take a mouth, any mouth, we're all waiting for you'. But then I'll realise that's not the most in-tune way to go about it and start looking inside me for what we really want, what the still, small, voice of love and truth prompts towards. I find great use in the idea that our uneasiness, our pain, are the shadows that reveal the Light to us. Without shadows we cannot see the Light: they show us where it's coming from so we can turn towards it more fully, see what else it has to show us as we move into it, discovering the larger picture.

F16 Having been brought up in a Quaker family, I can't remember not

understanding how Meetings for Worship for Business were conducted. The Quaker business method has never puzzled me, and for years
it was the only way of getting through business that I was aware of. I
knew that other groups voted, but I knew nothing of the fast pace of
non-Quaker business meetings.

I belong because I understand the process: I feel that I am
knowledgeable about what is good practice and what is not. It goes
far deeper than this. I'm committed to the process we, as Quakers, use
in order to move forward with our decisions. I believe that when used
well, it is an amazingly faithful way to move forward. To describe how
my commitment plays itself out is more difficult. Am I guilty of
sitting and fuming when things don't seem to be going well, when
Friends speak for too long or repeat points already expressed? I'm not
someone who comes out with short sentences of received wisdom
and clearness. I've not (yet) got involved with trying to teach Friends
better practice of the Quaker business method.

Yet I feel a strong commitment to ensuring that we continue to
practise our method of conducting Quaker business. It is in our
actions that we make a statement about our faith. Our practice of the
Quaker business method says many things about what we believe
about equality: in letting all speak; in not overriding the dissenting
voice(s), in believing that we're all capable of speaking the will of
godde. Whether we believe that the phrase 'will of godde' means
seeking the will of the Divine, or searching for the Truth, or simply
searching for the best way forward for us as a group, is less important. What is important is that we are not committed to furthering
our own personal desires and wishes, but to moving forward in a
deeper unity.

F17 I don't think we interrogate the idea of 'the will of God' enough. Is it
something we are uncovering, or is it the process of our discernment
rather than the outcome that is 'the will of God'? And if we disagree
on this fundamental aim/purpose of the business meeting, how can
we hold a Meeting for Worship for Business in right ordering? I

sometimes wonder if discerning the will of God is a myth, and it is more a question of egos, logic and a little bit of creativity in a hotpot of resolution and 'ways forward'. Sometimes I do sense the deep conviction of someone in the meeting 'prompted to love and truth' and I know that God is in our midst. Is God always there? Is God's presence essential? Is it enough to say that when two or three are gathered in God's name, we have a worshipful gathering, discerning the will of God?

I often believe the responsibility expected of each individual in a business meeting is too great. It's easy to fall into the trap of thinking that we are being expected to be experts on everything from legal systems, accountancy, architecture, furniture, children, drugs and genetic engineering to international relations, in order to make an informed decision. Meeting for Sufferings seems to me to be a victim of this attitude. We need to remember that theocratic does not mean democratic (where everyone has to have a voice), and that it needs to entail devolved responsibility, if only for more specialised or trivial areas. We are bad at letting go and delegating successfully.

Because of this, we spend a lot of time and energy in meetings for church affairs and a lot of money on expenses. My commitment to acting on the promptings to love and truth makes me want to spend less time in committee meetings and to use Quakerism as a base point rather than an ending point. The Religious Society of Friends seems to take an awful lot of self-maintenance. It seems to me that the system is old-fashioned in its use of time; it's not designed for the frenzied busy-ness of the materialistic 1990s, in which Quakers as much as others are subjected to demands at the workplace and at home, the working week is longer, and child-care is no longer the responsibility of the servants. In theory, such a strong, committed base should enable us to act more vigorously on the promptings of the Spirit. Sometimes, though, our energies get absorbed in ensuring the base is still there. There is a task for the group, the job of maintaining the group, and the process by which the group attacks the task, and the edges of those things get confused and blurred. We seem to expend our energies on maintenance and process rather than on the task.

Can you think of any solutions to the time problem?

How about delegation, education in the best use of the business method and personal discipline? How do Friends learn to keep to the point, to speak concisely and to be tactful all the time? **P7**.

F18 Do you see Divinity as immanent – as here and now and in me and in you and in the world? If godde is truly immanent, doesn't that give us a lot of responsibility? We are truly their 'hands and feet'. All the more reason for listening very carefully to the still, small voice inside.

See **B1** *for a description of what someone hears.*

G Truth, Honesty and Integrity

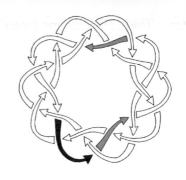

Truth, Honesty and Integrity

What is the nature of our commitment to truth and honesty?

Truth is the route of our action.	**G2.**
We must be honest with ourselves…	**G4.**
…and with others.	**G3.**
Living truthfully means more than simply not lying.	**G8, G9.**
Tensions can arise between a commitment to being honest and a commitment to being loving.	**G12.**
A commitment to honesty, to truth, means that we must continually question ourselves and others.	**G15, H1.**

G Truth, Honesty and Integrity

G1 What are you committed to in your spiritual practice?

I am committed to picking blackberries, to the freedom of wasps, spiders and ladybirds, to the water in the lake. I am committed to being *aware* of the universal self, to trying to express the life and essence of the world around us. I am committed to waiting for inspiration and discernment, rather than passively accepting what is given to me by any particular tradition, and to finding out who I am and where I come from.

I am committed to taking responsibility for my own spirituality and emotional maturity, to my passion, to loving, to those I care about and to myself, to seeking, to my sense of curiosity (science and spirit), to prayer and meditation and to living the way I feel is *right*.

Everything has its inherent mystery and mystical properties.

The writer of **C13** *believes in the inherent magic in everyone.*

G2 The ways we interact with each other and with the world must be rooted in love and truth; we may not always be able to reconcile all our beliefs on how to act on this. Engaging with the world is a messy business, which often forces us to compromise our absolute values if we are to achieve anything. This does not mean that these values are worthless or that lying is unproblematic, but rather that we need to be actively and attentively loving in our lives; in order to belong to our community of all people we need to be as truthful as possible.

Can we belong to a community of all people? See **L1**, **P8**.

G3 We shouldn't forget the power of our obligation to speak the truth to those who lie, just as we must love those who hate us. We need to think of the consequences of our actions and whether they are truthful. Without a commitment to truth and to seriously involving ourselves, we cannot belong fully to the wider community.

Sometimes we may have to sacrifice some of this sense of belonging for the sake of acting on deeper truths, but this should not be done lightly. Belonging and being committed to the world-wide family of all people is not just a privilege, it is also a calling and a responsibility.

G4 We are called to meet that of godde in others; for this we have to involve that of godde in ourselves, which we hide by being anything but truthful. Similarly, our obligation to engage with our world's social structures and mechanisms can only be half realised when we are only half present. The concepts of witness and testimony are founded on openness and honesty, which must apply to the words we speak.

Clearly, lying about a late piece of schoolwork and about international arms deals with oppressive regimes in foreign countries are not the same. But any division of the world into areas in which truth is or isn't necessary is false and dangerous. Still, is telling lies of whatever kind so important beyond the specific context? Does telling day-to-day lies really undermine our commitment to truth? Of course I think it does, even more so when it is done unthinkingly or uncaringly.

Not lying is by no means the only form of truth and I don't believe it's the most important kind. Loving our neighbours and trying to act in their best interests is vital, and, as I said earlier, being honest is integral to this.

Loving our neighbours, even when they are far away,... **N14**.

G5 Waiving our commitment to Truth for whatever reason involves individualising truth and claiming it as something which we must keep separate from some part of the community to which we belong. Thus we separate ourselves from the community and, if we are not careful, divide the world into the secular and the sacred.

Sometimes we may feel that the splits in the world community and the oppositions we face in our attempts at living truthfully render this meaningless, and that we are crippling ourselves if we are naïve enough to be truthful.

The sacred/secular divide... see **N11**.

G6   Sincerity may be better than commitment: it is more realistic in its lack of expectations of the future. The future is uncertain and largely out of our control (why else do we say when setting the time of our next meeting 'if nothing occurs to prevent'?). If we were more sincere and sensitive to the consequences of our actions, it would allow us to be more flexible and open to change.

G7   For several years I have not wanted to commit myself to any religion or pressure-group, although I have pretty well committed myself to a career. I need earning power soon so I can afford the freedom to study religions until I am perfectly happy with my choice.

Maybe I will never choose. Maybe I will spend my whole life searching – what a romantic picture!

G8   In our Quaker traditions truth means a great deal more than 'not-lies'. Truth involves trying to see the true nature of things and to recognise godde's will in the world.

Being truthful is active, and involves going beyond our selves to see the world in the light of what we know of godde.

Being truthful has also meant speaking only the truth, which is a difficult idea for me, in that I do not feel confident or knowledge-able enough to be able to locate firm boundaries of truth; indeed, I suspect there aren't such boundaries.

Living truthfully with others... **L1**.

G9   The issue of lying, when we say what we believe to be untrue, is another order of 'apartness from godde'. I have lied many times to avoid awkward situations, and I know this is a fundamental falling short of my testimony to truth and I feel it hinders me from belonging to the wider community. The issue of truth for us as Quakers is at least partly one of identity. Being truthful means being honest about who we are, individually and in whatever groups we belong to.

In withholding truths or telling falsehoods we place a barrier between ourselves and others. It is hard to love across such barriers because they prevent us from being wholly present. Our place in a family of all people requires us to (aspire to) engage deeply and lovingly with whoever we meet: difficult enough anyway, near impossible when we don't involve our true selves.

G10 It seems to me that in the past there was some sort of truth that was absolute, or at least people perceived it as such. Maybe that's what leads to wars and burnings though. The only truth I know is the truth of how I feel, where I have been and how it was for me. Sticking to that is hard enough in a world that seems to consist mainly of polite and social lies.

G11 We [as Quakers] have a commitment to the truth of our experience. At one level, this means I find it scarier to be arrested on protests, because I don't feel able to lie about my name and thus avoid prosecution, or to jump trains or buses, because it's stealing, or to lie on forms in order to have a hassle-free life.

G12 There are times when telling the truth would cause hurt and seems like an unloving act.

Withholding the truth when we know that it will hurt the person we tell, because we don't want to be the bearer of bad tidings, is a horribly selfish thing to do. In my experience it is loads 'less worse' to be told the (hurtful) truth by someone who loves you than to be 'the last to know'.

I have also been in a situation in which I had to break my word to someone with regard to a confidence they had told me, because I couldn't cope with the consequences of not talking about it – that the awful things going on would continue. I broke my word to keep my integrity.

It is this sort of situation in which I find my commitment to truth and honesty most difficult to maintain.

G13 One of the ways we can break down barriers is by regarding others' truths as valid, as they are based on another's personal experience, which cannot be doubted.

> *Why don't we doubt others' experiences?*
> *Can there be an objective Truth?*
>
> *Does anyone have the right to judge our commitment?* **N20**.

G14 I'll say what I want, write what I want and do it how the fuck I want to. What are you going to say to that, eh? I hope that most readers would resist the temptation to condemn my foul language and try to understand a little. I know that it's not big and not clever, but I'm not either – I don't mean to cause any offence, but I was dragged up swearing – just as you may have been brought up on a diet of meaningful adjectives. True godliness don't turn anyone out of the world.

> *How does the language we use relate to our personal identity?*
> *Is there unity behind such a variety of forms of expression?* See **E15**.

G15 I still struggle with some practices and attitudes I find amongst Friends. I am still surprised and shocked even, but I suppose what we find is our common humanity, with all its individual foibles. The key is never to give up, and especially not to cease questioning, for that would imply either surrender, complete satisfaction or death.

> *See* **E16**.

Many of us find security in holding on to what we know. We can be stuck in our lack of commitment and our inability to place trust in another. Our independence, whilst being a very valuable thing, can also be a barrier to new relationships.

What if we don't know what we are holding on to? See **H8**.

The writer of **H5** *took the plunge!*

I am continually trying, reassessing, striving to get things right, becoming able to focus on what's fundamentally important by self-enquiry.

Committing oneself to a continual process? **H13**.

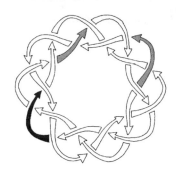

Personal Identity

How does your spiritual path shape your identity?

I am committed to the spiritual path in my heart and in my head, and my feet are walking on it, in contact with the earth. Within Quakers I contribute my money, my time and my energy. I made the decision (commitment) to become a member, but I am also a member of the Pagan Federation, which involves money, time and energy as well.

This Friend appears to be comfortable with two identities.
What about the writer of **H4***?*

My commitment consists of daily meditation, reminding myself of my vision and trying to act on it. That is the practical side of it. The sense of commitment is a sense of longing for the Truth. This longing seems to be my motivation.

H1 *talks of a commitment to honesty.*

Section G *is called 'Truth, Honesty and Integrity'.*
You might find it an interesting exploration of Truth.

H *Personal Identity*

H1   Part of my Quaker commitment to honesty and integrity, is challenging myself about my values and behaviour. One of the parts of my life in which I have had to completely re-evaluate what I do, what I believe, what I assume, is my physical love/sensuality. As a consequence of reading (mainly feminist) literature reflecting alternative culture and talking to friends, I came to realise that I had learnt an alienated idea of sexuality from society around me. This view of the erotic as something 'banished to the bedroom and used as a vehicle for exploitation, control and abuse' (Zoe White, 1992) seems to me to be an apartness from godde.

I regard one of my primary goals in life as participating in the work of creating the 'Kingdom of Heaven', a society in Christ's image, from the visions of our souls. Living inside the flow of divine love, washing the accumulations of other people's assumptions from my eyes, I am learning a new way of holding relationships rightly. It is difficult at times because the Love in me is having to carve new channels, and it is very much easier to slip into older, less *right* ones. I feel I have become tender, raw on the outside, and I become afraid that people will misinterpret my actions. I cannot doubt though, that I am truly led in my aspirations, in my commitment to mutually empowering relations, to fusing the physicality of love with the emotional, mental ideas of godde.

G4 reminds us of the concepts of witness and testimony.

H2   I could feel as if there are two parts of me. 'I' am made up of a soul plus a body, who courted and were married during my conception, gestation and birth. This is the foundation of my primary commitment — myself. There are both responsibilities and privileges: in return for inspiring my body with, as the Great Mother Charge puts it, 'knowledge of the spirit eternal', my soul receives an incarnation in time, with sensory experience. My body gains the security of a 'personal Jesus' for its 'duty to feel' — joy, pain, anger, comfort, grief, loneliness, communion. My body is the child, the little sister, the younger partner of my soul.

A mystical view of the world leads me to see that I am not just the body that moves around. Molecules that were part of me are everywhere I have been, and the stuff I am made of has been in this universe forever. I am aware of my soul extending forth from my body to all I care about, and I could hardly escape knowing that my health and well-being depend on the people and the eco-systems around me. So what sounds ultimately selfish – 'I am primarily committed to myself' – leads my view outwards to realising that I am more than myself.

H3   These sugar candy chains
Wrapped around me
Not constricting
But chains I myself chose
And made of daisies
Belonging
In comforting arms
Enveloped
Supported and carried
Way over rocks
To safety on Life's sunny shore
Without Commitment
Intertwined and symbiotic
Like a bromeliad
On an Amazonian tree.

H4   I am not Black. I am not White. I am neither one nor the other. In my more positive moments, I know I should feel that I am part of two cultures, instead of between two, but the truth is, I rarely feel positive about my race. I am very aware that politically (in England at any rate) I am considered to be black, simply because I am not white. Is it right to define somcone's identity by what they are not?

Language is a big stumbling block for me. Take an equal

opportunities section on a job application or other official form. Nowadays, there is usually a wide range of races given from which to choose your racial origin. Almost all the forms give the instruction 'Tick one box only'. Those of us who are more than one race are usually supposed to tick 'Other – please specify'. Is it surprising that I feel I belong to neither of the two cultures my parents came from, when I am forced to identify myself as 'other'? I am made to feel rejected, unwanted and unacceptable by society. In actual fact, aren't I, and thousands like me, the ultimate expression of racial integration?

As a child at primary school, I remember being called a 'Paki'. My father was most unhelpful about the issue and told me that the kids who called me that were just ignorant, and I was better than that. My mother explained to me what a 'Paki' was and what my racial origins are, in the hope that I would have a reply to racist taunts. But I learned to keep as quiet as possible about my racial background and to try to hide it. I wished that I was white. How many other non-white children wish that they were white, to stop the taunts and to feel like everybody else? I am not alone in having these feelings.

At the Quaker secondary school I went to, there was one incident, repeated many times during the seven years I was there, that still riles me. I would often get the message 'Your mother is in Central Hall'. Naturally I would be excited, and concerned, since my mother worked full-time a long way from my school and only an emergency would have brought her there of an evening. I would rush to Central Hall to find only the typing teacher, the *Asian* typing teacher.

During the Gulf War, whilst I was at university, I was thrown out of a phone box and told I was 'a fucking Iraqi' and to 'get back to where you belong'. I ran away and cried. Where do I belong?

Although uncomfortable with my racial identity in England (being labelled black because I am not white), I found it harder in India. There I was white, because I am not black. In England, being in the racial minority means that you are looked down on and made to feel inferior. In India, I felt that the opposite was true. Apart from being taken for a ride because I was obviously a tourist, I was treated with more respect and politeness because I was of the white minority. This made me feel more uncomfortable because of my feelings towards the imperialism of the British.

Junior Yearly Meeting (JYM) in 1988 was about race and racial issues. I remember there being only three of us who were not white, and it was then that it hit me that, for all its clear beliefs and commitments to equality, Quakers in Britain did not constitute a multi-racial society. What did reassure me was the way young Friends felt that: '...racism is more complex than simply black and white – it is part of a wider problem of prejudice involving sexism and religious bigotry' (Epistle of JYM, 1988). This showed me that young Friends saw racism as something to be open about, discussed, acknowledged and overcome in the same way that sexism should be.

To me, countering racism is very similar to countering sexism. You are fighting a prejudice that is based on ignorance and fear, with no logical explanation or justification. This is why what I wanted, and still want, is a non-white space to openly share hopes, fears, thoughts and maybe tears about racial issues. I have always valued my time in a female-only space for this kind of thing, and I long for the time when I will be able to experience something similar to do with racism.

I have been told, by someone I consider to be a feminist, that the Fellowship of Black Friends and their Families, never mind the idea of a non-white space, is a divisive thing and is trying to create differences that don't exist. Being blind to differences is as hurtful as being aggressive because of differences.

Sometimes, I feel that things are not moving on in the slightest. I have recently been talking to my eight year old niece about racism. Unlike me, she has felt proud of having Indian blood in her. She tells people, and she thinks it's great. And she has suffered because she is open about it. We discussed it for quite some time, and tried to work out why people at school aggressively and teasingly call her a Red Indian and why I was called a Paki. We are trying to understand what other people feel and what leads them to say and do the things that they do. Are enough white people considering the same?

For the record, my mother is white/English and my father was black/South Indian. I have always lived in England and have only visited India twice.

H5   All my life I have been hampered by problems with my racial origin. Through examining my feelings for this lecture, I have finally, after 25 years of ignoring and being scared to look at race issues, begun to look at my sense of belonging in racial terms as well as in other physical terms. It is totally enlightening. I feel great, I feel proud, at long last, to be half Indian, not ashamed, not constantly trying to forget it all. I am hungry to know more about myself and my roots.

H6   I am committed to my creativity and to encouraging and respecting creativity in others.

H7   I have made a pact with myself to discover what love is. I am committed to my curiosity.

H8   Sometimes I feel like a little girl with a fairy-tale fantasy about true love and magic. I feel that I don't know the 'rules' of relationships, how much to give and take, how to communicate my desires, but hope that somehow we will fit together without pain, that we will be a perfect match. Commitment is easy in this unreal world.

Sometimes I feel like a mature woman, sexually experienced, desirous, passionate, loving, articulate about my emotions, assertive about who I am and what I need, growing from difficulty and challenge. Commitment is petrifying. How can I be part of someone else's life and how can I make someone part of mine when I am an individual, not a couple? Commitment means compromise, change, working together, opening up, being vulnerable, suffering – yet it is also joy, pleasure, closeness, the satisfaction of being joined and connected to someone.

Marriage seems like the fairy-tale fantasy in this context. It is not something I expect to happen to me. Marriage is for life. I would not face those vows lightly. If I cannot make them, I would prefer to be in relationships which are committed and long-term, which do not have the cruel expectation of lifelong happiness.

Is marriage the 'cruel expectation of lifelong happiness'?
*The writer of **J18** doesn't think so.*

H9 in my innocence i committed my body
i was young it was all i could give him
he made me think i was special
he made me belong
i belonged to him –

i craved intimacy and understanding
he offered rApE and AbUsE
to avoid loneliness in desperation
i committed myself to him –

he made me promise nOt tO tEll
not to tell my teachers not to tell my friends
not to tell my parents not to tell his wife

so in my lonely hours
i shed many tears
i prayed that the spirit
would take away my fears

many years later i gathered the strength
i told my lovers i told my friends
i told my parents i told the police

the police weren't interested
'it was too long ago'
'not enough evidence to show'

H Personal Identity

it was nearly too much
but the spirit was there
now i understand who really cares

i belong to no-one –
i'm committed to me –

Rape Crisis helplines are in local telephone books.
The London Rape Crisis Centre number is 0171 837 1600.
The Samaritans' number is 0345 90 90 90.

H10 I have been suffering with pain in my joints for a while. There is nothing like constant pain. I have always thought that the concept of pain as a teacher was a bit masochistic, but I have learnt differently. I was sitting, crying, in my bed, unable to think about what to do with myself except keep warm, and I had a really profound mystical sense of my soul in me, as a part of godde whose attention was Totally in Me, and who Loved me and cared with me and for me. And that was the fulfilment of godde's part of my commitment to incarnation, that in my suffering, as in my joy, I was not alone.

H11 Indian Summer

In youth, it was a way I had
To do my best to please,
And change, with every passing lad,
To suit his theories.

But now I know the things I know,
And do the things I do;
And if you do not like me so,

To hell, my love, with you!

Dorothy Parker (Morgan, 1996)

This poem is important to me because it illustrates that the true meaning of commitment in relationships is being true to yourself. It is more important to be true to yourself and committed to your beliefs than to just try to fit in with other people, particularly your partner.

Being honest with yourself is important to the writer of **J16**.

H12 Dearest Matt,

It's nine months now since we jumped the Beltane fire and promised to commit ourselves to one another for a year and a day. It seemed a daunting prospect at the time, and we entered that tryst with a justifiable amount of fear running beneath our excitement and joy. Our love was so huge, though, that we felt we could approach our inevitable difficulties with a truthful eye and an open heart. I haven't looked back on that jump for a while. We were so full of each other and our new relationship, so wantonly joyful. There's little to compare with the rush of new-born love, and to begin with such a dedicated commitment was the biggest thing I've done to date.

I'm still rushing, even now. We've had a good few troubles to deal with between us since May. Is life always so challenging? There are times when I feel that I'll lose my mind if I can't have a week when there isn't some new crisis to deal with. You have it even harder than I do, with your ever multiplying responsibilities – a different hat to assume for each hour of every day. It shouldn't upset me that we are each often beset by anger, exhaustion, despair, low sex-drive, inattention and selfishness. Sometimes these things are cruelly synchronised and our support structure terribly strained. These times feel very hard to deal with. It is difficult to identify which problems are caused by external pressures and which are related to our relationship.

Am I the only person who finds it more difficult to find words for the best times than for the worst? When I'm in full bounce, I don't need to have any words, because the feeling is so entire that describing it would be irrelevant. At other times, it would be so nice to have that feeling on paper to reflect back on, as a reminder of what I can achieve. Still, as you were saying a few weeks ago, what matters most is the middle time, when we live our lives with adequate attention to those things which fall outside of our relationship, assisting each other to reach our goals creatively and supportively. I'm really glad to be able to say that these times, for me, form the foundation of my loving you. (This feels a bit like writing a c.v.!)

I hate it when you're overwhelmed with worries. (Of course, when I'm in that situation, I find it hard to try and assess its impact on you: it's all too immediate.) You seem so tortured sometimes that nothing touches you. It's hard to try and love you then, because it seems so insignificant. I'm so unable to provide an answer. A lot of my struggle with this is becoming easier, as I begin to really understand that it's not my place to take it all away from you. In previous relationships, I've tried to assume that burden. It wouldn't fit on my back, and I collapsed under its weight. I emerged crushed, beaten by my own perceptions of my responsibility to the relationship. My commitment to you does not include that as part of the job description. I will willingly share joint responsibility, and undertake tasks which are within my capabilities and beyond yours. But I promise to remain faithful to myself, and love myself as much as I love you, and know the boundaries of my needs, abilities and commitments, and apply them to our relationship.

At a Young Friends gathering, sometime between last May and now, someone was saying that you can't have commitment without a sense of belonging, and I agree with that in many circumstances. I don't, however, know where it fits in our relationship. Do we belong to each other? I find that difficult to conceive of; it can't be right. Do we belong with each other? At the moment, we fit well together. I hope we will continue to do so for some time. But belonging with each other seems too exclusive as a phrase. It seems to cut out the rest of our lives and separate them from something which appears to be a fixed unit, like a pair of shoes. You can't make use of one without the other.

I don't want to be useless without you. I know I am not. When we decide to change the state of our relationship, there will not be a part of me which is irrevocably lost: I will have a unique set of experiences in my lexicon which have been part of my growth and development. I can, on the other hand, qualify the content of my commitment to you. I knew at the Beltane fire that I didn't really know what I was leaping into. We knew too little about each other for that. I did know that I would have to learn about your scars and show you mine. I knew that we would inflict and receive new wounds, although I hoped they would be few and heal quickly.

Living truthfully, to me, will inevitably involve some pain, and there are times, like now, when it hurts and hurts. I hope hard that it might imply that we are learning, not just bashing each other with rocks. What I'm committed to is having a relationship which is truthful, not hurtful, which inspires openness to the world, but which will offer protection in extremes.

I'm committed to exploring myself and becoming greater, more essential and less dispersed. I am voluntarily devoted to you. I'm committed to building a family and community life which has you and your daughter as focus points. I want to be a wise woman. Your amazing ideas, your clarity of mind and the way you love the world are helping me to acquire wisdom. These things help to persuade me that our commitment is solid and positive. I doubt and vacillate, but my commitment never wavers. Even when I need to be away from you, it still feels strong, and though my love doesn't always feel the same, it's always there.

With love

H13   Love never fails. But… where there is knowledge, it will pass away. For we know in part, and we prophesy in part… Now we see but in a glass darkly; but then face to face. Now I know in part; then I shall know fully, even as I am fully known. (1 Corinthians 13, v. 8-12)

I love in order to know better. I commit myself in order to learn. It is not possible to look from a place of non-commitment and understand fully and then commit – as if I could sit down and calculate whom I should marry and consider the matter concluded. We commit ourselves, first, to a process of 'coming to know'. That is why 'belief in God', as the phrase is often used, is a misleading expression. It sounds like 'belief in the theory of evolution', assent to a fixed set of propositions for which reasons can be given. But people who say they believe in God will also explain how their ideas about God have changed dramatically over time, acknowledge their inability to give complete reasons for their beliefs and maintain that this does not matter.

The end of the process of growing love and knowledge is to 'see face to face'. Try to comprehensively describe the face of someone you know to someone else: it's impossible. We recognise faces, we want to see faces; thinking of a person is thinking of his or her face. Faces are 'intangibles': we know them, we recognise them, but we cannot describe them. Moreover, when face to face with a person, we become most aware of her uniqueness, a uniqueness which means that we will never fully know or understand her. Thomas Aquinas did not believe that the 'knowledge that we could never know God' was possessed before he started to think about or contemplate God, for that would have meant that the whole approach to God was useless. He did discover, however, that it was the 'ultimate knowledge', the face-to-face knowledge of the inexpressible and unknowable face.

I cannot define love, but I do not consider the word useless.

Is love central to all we do? **P8**.

H14

Our deepest fear is not that we are inadequate.
Our deepest fear is that we are powerful beyond measure.
It is our light, not our darkness, that most frightens us.
We ask ourselves, 'Who am I to be brilliant, gorgeous, talented,
fabulous?'
Actually, who are you not to be? You are a child of God.
Your playing small doesn't serve the world.
There's nothing enlightened about shrinking so that other
people won't feel insecure around you.
We are all meant to shine, as children do.
We were born to manifest the glory of God that is within us.
It's not just in some of us; it's in everyone.
And as we let our own light shine, we unconsciously give other
people permission to do the same.
As we're liberated from our own fear, our presence automatically
liberates others.

Nelson Mandela, from his inauguration speech as President of
South Africa.

This illustrates to me how important it is to feel good about yourself
and have faith in what you are capable of. We are all powerful if we
let ourselves fulfil our potential, and I carry these words wherever I
am, to give me strength when I feel low.

There is another extract about being committed to yourself at **J16**.

Who do we think we are? **P9**.

Relationships in which there is little direct communication about the relationship itself can often be ambiguous and insecure. There is a fear that we do not know our own desires well enough, particularly when we are out of touch with ourselves. Taking the plunge to commit can deepen the relationship and enable it to blossom in an environment of stability and security. On the other hand, if the motivation to commit is to escape the insecurity and stress of independence, it can have a negative effect on our spiritual growth. Security can encourage complacency and the relationship being taken for granted.

> We need to be clear about our meanings of the word 'commitment' in a relationship... **J11**.

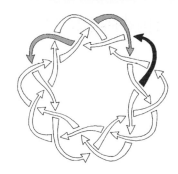

Friendship, Love and Sexuality

Should we be afraid of commitment?

Our fears over commitment could be similar to those we have over lack of commitment. Sometimes we can be reassured by the commitments we have, being able to rely upon them when facing choices and decisions. Our commitments can provide a framework that enables us to make sense of the mess and confusion of life and help us to keep hold of our identity. Thus our commitment to a spiritual discipline can enable us to have greater freedom. Our commitment to honesty and integrity and to trying to see things as they really are leads to clarity.

*Friendship and sexual relationships... **J12**.*

Not committing yourself to something is often to commit yourself to something else, or to close doors to yourself (such as having children). It can lead to inconsistency and an inability to get to the root of things.

J15 *talks about closing doors.*

J   Friendship, Love and Sexuality

J1   I believe that all interpersonal relationships are intrinsically sacramental and therefore an outward expression of inward grace/spirituality/divinity. Interpersonal relationships are in a way (an outward expression? embodiment?) a manifestation of finding 'that of godde' in another person.

J2   We are privileged to participate in so sacred a relationship as friendship. We can 'use the experience and concept of friendship as a paradigm for mutual relation, for justice in the small daily places of our lives as well as an image for justice and "godding" in the world. Nothing matters more.' (Heyward, 1989)

> *Do we remember often enough that our friendship is a form of social action? You could go to* **N13** *or* **J4**.
>
> *'godding' in the world...* **N12**.

J3   To have a friendship which grows in depth and understanding requires several commitments, the first being to try. To try to understand, to try to be open, to be willing to learn about ourselves and each other and to accept the other and their feelings. To try to sort things out when they go wrong, when there is an argument, for example, is also part of friendship, not simply to give up the minute there is a problem, even when we are experiencing great pain.

To stick by someone – a friend – when they are in trouble is also part of a good friendship. All these things demand commitment and dedication, as well as the involvement, fun and laughter which should also be part of friendships. An example from my own life: I phoned a friend because I was upset, saying I'd come over to him when he said did I need to talk. He wasn't there when I got there; I waited, left, came back. He was there then. He'd ridden the five miles to my house, waited there for me. And although we spent so much of that evening missing each other, the commitment/dedication is not something one finds in everyone. The same friend, on another occasion when I was feeling upset again and phoned, came over at midnight to see if I was OK. And when I think of a committed personal relationship, that's one of the ones I think of.

4 I find particular significance in our name, the Religious Society of Friends. I feel that friendship should form the basis of how we relate to the world that we live in, whether the relationship formed is a passing acquaintance, a long-term friendship or one with nature and the environment. In the way that I live and treat those around me, I do my best to recognise 'that of God' in all that lives and all that is created.

Is this what **N5** *is about?*

5 What does commitment entail in a friendship context? Friendship is about honesty and candour, while at the same time respecting each other's space. Sharing is by choice. Our close (sexual) relationships can be suffocating and inflexible, but our friendships can feel unstable and unreliable. Acceptance and belonging are important to both. But also, unconditional love would imply the willingness to give space to your partner to grow, and to let them go if necessary to allow them to break the 'belonging' bond.

Can commitment and belonging be separate? **P2**.

6 Sexual relationships are not to me intrinsically different in terms of commitment from any other relationship – the level of commitment should not differ, but the nature of the commitment is different. The most important thing in a relationship is that the expectations are openly talked about – what these are should and does vary hugely depending on the individuals and combination of individuals involved in the relationship. Often the level of commitment in a relationship can unfortunately be ignored as an issue, until the assumed commitment is stretched beyond what is acceptable to one member in the relationship.

Different people see commitment in relationships in different ways… see **J11**.

J7 Space
Space   –
edges   and
the   places   in   between.

Seen,   or   unseen   –
walls   and   screens   and   boundaries   –
or   bridges?

Safe   places   –
my   space,
your   space,
our   spaces   when   there's
nothing   in   between.

Picture   the   scene.
A   room.
Your   room.
A   chair   perhaps,   a   table.
And   candles   lit   like   eyes   of
people   that   you   long   for,
Belong   for.

A   room.
Your   room.
Where   you   watch   the   candles,
but   the   door's   ajar.
And   at   some   future   time   –
Not   now,   not   necessarily   now   –
There   might   be   space,
There   might   be   grace,
to   show   another   person   around   the   room.

Your   room.
And   light   more   candles.
To   show   him   what   you   know   or   think   you   know.
To   show   him   without   show.
Yes or no?

8 How do you know whether someone is committed to you? Does it matter? Should one worry about it?

Commitment is tricky. I can be close friends with a woman and not be sure whether it's romantic love or a deep friendship. The distinction for me is our boundary in relation to physical contact and whether the relationship is exclusive in its closeness. Often each person has a different view of the type of relationship it is, and it throws up some shadows which make 'normal' interactions into painful ones.

9 With regard to recognising commitment as a community, there has been some uncertainty in our Young Friends group as to why we choose to formally celebrate commitments to sexual relationships (through weddings and meetings for commitment) and recognise commitments to organisations (through membership), but not other forms of commitment, such as friendship or commitment to our values and testimonies.

10 I was wondering about the difference between friends and lovers. Or rather – is there really a difference? Or is it just a barrier, a block that is put up in order to compartmentalise our lives a little more? Lovers, especially as a relationship grows, often want a definite commitment, a spoken agreement, but friends rarely expect or demand that. And, in my life, looking at my close friendships, there are very few people with whom I haven't been sexual at some point, and even if I haven't been, often the potential is/has been there. Yet my sexual friendships don't demand 'heavy' commitment either. It's only when getting into primary relationships that the issue comes up.

11 What is it that makes me feel committed to my primary partner? And what happens if she doesn't think or feel that I'm committed to her? She says that, for her, commitment has to include 'faithfulness', i.e. for us to be monogamous, and probably a more definite time commitment so that we'd see each other more often. For me, my commitment to her is about the way I love her, that I'm honest with her. Yes, I have other lovers/sexual partners. I think my relationships with them enhance, rather than disrupt, my relationship with her. My commitment is in the way and frequency with which I think about her, in the fact that all my other lovers know that my main relationship is with her.

Does commitment imply exclusivity? Look at **L7**.

J12   I know, from my own experience, that being very close to several people, whether sexually or not, doesn't lessen the intimacy of my feelings for any one of those people. The unquestioned assumptions of compulsory monogamy have always puzzled me. I have never expected any one person to fulfil all my needs, wants or desires. My many friends offer many different qualities and wonderful experiences. And this is a common experience with most people. I don't then expect one lover/sexual relationship to offer the full diversity of qualities and wonderful experiences. My lovers are also my friends.

I often find that to enter into a sexual relationship with someone who is already a friend enhances the friendship, offering new insights into that person, sometimes bringing us closer in a way that would have been very unlikely without the sexual contact. I don't see that as breaking the trust of someone I'm already having an ongoing relationship with. This is partly because I am open and honest about this with everyone involved, and partly because my feelings for individuals are rarely affected by my feelings for any other person: being sexual with someone new doesn't mean I have less love/fondness for someone I am already being sexual with. However, I'm justifying myself and I needn't. My experience has commonly been that meeting new sexual/potentially sexual partners needn't diminish feelings of love and commitment to ongoing lovers/partners.

It was at 22 that I moved into a definite awareness of what

this meant to me, to my life. Previously my sexuality hadn't been particularly entwined with my spirituality, although I had some guilt when first becoming explicitly sexual because of biblical/Christian ideals. That something which enhanced intimacy and closeness so much, as well as being fun and exciting, could be disapproved of by a Divine Being is something I will probably never understand.

Currently I am leading a happy, fulfilled, enjoyable life filled with many different people; some are friends, some are sexual partners, some are both, and this changes. I love a few people very deeply and strongly; my love for each is independent of my love for others. There are many people with a special and unique place in my life/heart. I have no intention of belonging to any of them, individually or collectively, but I feel that I belong in my lifestyle. When I had newly chosen to live in a completely honest, non-monogamous way, I felt liberated: for the first time I was living life in the way that I wanted. I was very clear that however difficult others found me, I would be up front about my needs and desires. At the time, I wasn't sure how this would work out, but I can now say that I feel far more at peace with myself, with my loved ones, with my godde, having made that commitment to honesty in my sexuality.

13 Living, as I do, as an openly non-monogamous bisexual woman, I have some similarities with many different communities. I belong very much in the poly-amorous, bisexual community, and feel strongly that I am most able to be close to poly-amorous, bisexual people. I have been clear that I don't want to be seen to belong to the heterosexual community. I resent the assumption that, if I'm with a man, I must be heterosexual, although, interestingly, I rarely resent being seen as a lesbian if I'm with a woman. Nevertheless, I have walked, alone, around Lesbian and Gay Pride wanting to shout 'I'm bisexual, I'm not lesbian'. For a time I was attending two groups, one a secular bisexual women's group, the other a Quaker lesbian group. I felt a far greater sense of belonging to the Quaker lesbian group, despite that difference in sexualities, than I did to the secular bisexual women's group. My spirituality is such a crucial part of my sexuality, of my identity.

Do we see people by one or more of their labels, or as a whole? **L3**.

London Lesbian and Gay Switchboard – 0171 837 7324
Bisexual Phoneline – 0181 569 7500

J14 Sex is an emotional experience. It can be exclusive, special, intimate, spiritual. It can also be fun, outrageous, pleasureful. When I have sex, I literally feel that I open myself to the person who I am with, becoming joined and connected to that person physically and emotionally. That openness entails vulnerability, and therefore trust is an essential part of it, otherwise there can be pain and power struggles. Sex means you know someone differently, it affects your relationship with them, adds an agenda, an intimacy. At the moment I want that intimacy to be exclusive, constant; I feel my feelings for my partner would be diminished if I had sex with someone else. And if my feelings weren't diminished, I would wonder whether the sex was worth it.

J15 Of course, not all, perhaps not even most, experiences of sex are positive. At 16 I was raped by someone I knew. The details of this are no longer important, the nightmares are subsiding, the numbness still haunts me, the anger is rife. Up until that day I'd never kissed anyone and sex had not entered my consciousness (I might have been a late developer).

It happened in my house, a safe place, while my parents were away. My reaction to this attack was to commit myself to silence. I could not and would not tell anyone. I felt confused, uncomfortable, embarrassed, humiliated, frightened. He told me that nobody would believe me, that I would be labelled a whore, that he would say I invited him in, that I seduced him, and that I wasn't even a good lay.

I felt small, insignificant, soiled, powerless. My body had let me down: I hadn't had the strength to fight. It was my fault. I even believed I somehow deserved this because my body had reacted to his touch.

I kept this commitment to silence for five years until I became so mad with anguish that I had to tell someone. So I did. It was so hard to talk – by then I'd convinced myself I was sick in the head, so warped that I'd dreamt this, made it up, imagined it. The listener did believe me, but I couldn't handle that so I retreated into myself again and didn't talk about it again for two years.

The other commitment I made that night was that sex would have no part in my life. I never again wanted to feel the way I had felt, I wanted to be a non-sexual being; sex was a bad thing, a dangerous thing, it was something other people did but not me. And so I grew up, left home, went to college, did a degree, worked, travelled, lived abroad, danced, partied, developed friendships. I became involved in Quakerism, politics, environmental issues. I read books, painted, lived each moment to the full. I filled my life with as much as I could, and although I occasionally kissed somebody, as soon as they looked at me in a sexual way or tried to touch me, I ran away. I grew and matured in all other aspects of my life, yet sexually I am still a little girl.

I thought I could get away with ignoring my sexuality, but recently I've begun to realise that things don't go away; maybe my commitment should have been to healing not hiding. Maybe sexuality is too big, too integral in all animals. I've also realised I am a sexual being whether I like it or not: I feel and I want and I can't deny it any more.

I'm scared, no terrified of changing, but I want to reclaim myself, to stop this man having control and power over me. I want to commit myself to healing and becoming whole. Who knows? – maybe I'll succeed.

The Samaritans – 0345 90 90 90.

J16 I have been having relationships with boys/men since I was about 14 – not always fully blown sexual relationships, but close 'boyfriend-girlfriend' relationships nevertheless. I had always presumed I was good at relationships. I have never had any problems attracting men and getting involved with them, but gradually I have begun to realise that things were not going as well as I had been letting myself believe. I was sitting in a bar in Portrush, Northern Ireland, with two of my best friends, having had a few drinks, when in the course of the conversation I said to them that I didn't have any male friends. I only realised the truth of this as I said it, and it shocked me. I had lots of acquaintances who were men, but none who I could call friends.

I gradually realised that this went some way to explaining why I only ever had very short relationships. In the last few years I'd had a whole string of relationships which all lasted between six and eight weeks. Before that night I had never noticed this pattern. I began to wonder if this was how long a relationship could last if it was built purely on physical attraction and not on friendship.

Throughout that summer this pattern became clearer in my head. I realised that the problem stemmed from my attitude to men. I have always wanted to settle down eventually into a permanent relationship with a man, partly because I very much want to have children. I discovered that I was categorising each man I met, putting him into one of two categories. He was either (a) a potential life partner and father of my children, or (b) not a potential life partner and therefore not worth bothering with. I wasn't seeing men as interesting individuals who might become my friends. I was unconsciously slotting them into roles and pretending that they fitted into the categories that I had created for them. By dismissing those in category (b) I was missing out on many potential friendships, but it was putting men into the category of potential life partners that was preventing me from having successful sexual relationships.

The pattern of my relationships went something like this. I would meet a man, we would be attracted to each other and begin a relationship. At the beginning it would work well and would often be very passionate, but things would start to go wrong. I would start to imagine this man as my long-term partner. I would imagine what sort of life we would have, imagine describing to our children how I met their father. This would be after knowing the man for only two or three weeks. I knew that if I talked like this to the man in question it would scare him off, so I would try to hide these feelings. I would convince myself that I was in love with him when I hardly knew him, but would try to act cool and detached when I was with him. The result was that I was giving out mixed signals, and the poor man got completely confused and backed off. The more he backed off the more I felt that I had to cling on, but also the more I felt that I could only keep him by playing it cool. I repeated this pattern over and over with lots of different men for a number of years.

I think that realising what was happening was the first step to doing something about it. The situation is now getting better because I can see it clearly and try and work out how to change it. I am still looking for a long-term partnership. I wish I could stop wanting that, but I can't just switch the feeling off. However, being conscious of my feelings does help me to make them more rational. I can look at a man now and think 'This is nice for now but it isn't something that will last forever', or ' This has potential but I don't know him well enough to think about anything long-term'. I still get those married with children fantasies, but by acknowledging them I can stop them controlling my actions.

There is one big success story to come out of this. Since I began to understand how I was categorising men, I have stopped ignoring those who I didn't see as potential partners. As a result I have made a number of men friends who I have since become very close to. This is a wonderful thing and I have gained a lot from these friendships. It is also a good sign with regard to my ability to make good sexual relationships. If I can have relationships built on genuine friendship then they have a much better chance of survival.

It's two years since that night in the pub in Portrush. My relationship patterns still haven't changed much. I still have relationships that fizzle out after a couple of months. I'm hoping that with the insight I've gained things should start to improve. I'm a lot more aware of my feelings now, and this must be a good thing. I still have a long way to go. There's still a lot more exploring and discovering to be done before I fully understand what is happening; maybe it's a lifelong process. However it turns out, I'm prepared for the struggle and I'm making progress.

Being honest about who you are... **G9**.

J17   One misty evening I came across my friend Jenny sitting at the bottom of her staircase in the cold quad, crying. Of course I asked her what was wrong. She told me it was something William had said – William was a rather good-looking young man she was beginning to feel a romantic interest in. He had come to her and asked her if she would be his girlfriend – and added that if she refused, he would commit suicide!

I took her to our friend's room and we comforted her as best we could, reassuring her that if she never wanted to see him again, we would protect her. She said she would sleep on it, and in the morning she decided to go on seeing William. In the end they got married, and live together happily, as far as I can tell.

To this day I do not know whether Jenny stays with William because she really wants to or because she is being kind to him. I feel strongly that the burden he has laid on her is unreasonable. She is trapped by his selfish passion. His declaration was in the best romantic tradition, but unfair nonetheless. What a difference there is between 'I would die for you!' and 'I will die without you!'

After I had written this, one of my friends asked me 'Why did you not get [psychiatric] help for William? He was dangerous! That would have been the way to protect Jenny, it would have removed the blackmail threat.' I remember that my attention at the time was all for Jenny, to protect her from the threatening man. Even now I can feel no sympathy for him. What a monster! If you love someone, shouldn't you consider their feelings too?

J18   Marriage has always puzzled me. I guess it's to do with a hang up I have about promises, a belief that you should never promise anything that you don't absolutely know you can keep. This after years of a father's empty promises – trips that never happened, gifts that never arrived, love that wasn't shown. I don't make promises I don't know I can keep – therefore, how could I get married?

And yet the idea of a life-long partner has always appealed to me. I always wanted to have a life-long monogamous relationship. It has never been so clear cut as to say I wanted it with a man; it was the monogamy that mattered. For a long time now I have seen marriage as a spiritual union – again this does not restrict it to a heterosexual relationship. I didn't see marriage as a legal, heterosexual, exclusive and negative entity, but rather a partnership of souls. If this is the important thing to me in a lifelong commitment, the gender of the partner is immaterial. I still believe that.

The enormity of having a child, and the responsibility that it brings, turned me off for some time. For me, the responsibility a parent has to their child is vast, huge, infinite maybe. I know that my feelings about children growing up and the support they need are not conventional, not 'normal', and I think that was another reason I couldn't commit myself to motherhood. I didn't have the head-space or energy to commit myself to enabling my child to develop their skills, their passions, their talents. I didn't feel I could give a child all the respect, nurturing, honesty, caring and loving they deserved, especially since I didn't feel sure that the father of my child would be likewise as committed to bringing up children in a positive, encouraging and enabling manner, not an ordering, telling and criticising way.

Two years ago, during the 1995 Summer Gathering, I went with a group of my friends (who happen to be wife, husband and daughter) to Meeting for Worship at Colthouse in the Lake District, where the couple had got married. The importance of the decision within the context of a relationship to have children overwhelmed me. The idea that, after years of trying not to get pregnant, my partner and

I would actively try to create a new being, someone separate from us to whom we had a responsibility, seemed to be the ultimate commitment. I have carried this with me ever since.

But then these things changed. While preparing for the Swarthmore Lecture I had to really think through these issues. How do I think I should commit myself to my child without stifling their creativity or preventing them from being an individual in their own right? What do I really believe about marriage? Is it really a promise that you guarantee to keep or is it something more?

My partner and I have been spending time learning how we now feel about our own childhood and each other's. Through this experience, we discovered a meeting of minds on how children should be respected and treated.

Then I looked again at the marriage promise. What I realised was that it is a promise about your journeys. You are not promising to stay with the person you marry for the rest of your life. You are promising to grow together and change together. I have (hopefully) years ahead of me. I will not be the same person at 56 as I am at 26. The marriage promise is a commitment to accepting we will not be the same person but wanting to change alongside each other.

We decided to have children before, as a couple, we decided to get married. The enormity of this decision was quite overwhelming. I was making at last the 'ultimate' commitment. We were not committing ourselves to each other, but to the child we wanted to have when we had a more dependable income. We had been living together for about six months, questioning our attitudes to marriage and commitment and the importance of spiritual matters, when this decision became apparent.

Then one morning we decided to get married. It turned out that we had each stopped thinking 'if we got married' and started thinking 'when' a few weeks earlier, but hadn't found the right moment to say so.

It was a very joyful, happy, yet awesome decision to take. And a change somehow took place. Someone had told me during Yearly

Meeting at Aberystwyth that although my partner and I were living together as if married, we weren't actually married and there was a definite difference. I didn't totally understand. I was surprised by this idea: we'd been living together, we'd decided to have children, why did the 'm' word make any difference? But it does. However much we thought we were committed before, we have taken that decision to make it public, and in a Meeting for Worship.

The force of rightness of the situation has come back to us over and over. After seeing the registrar, we were in a beautiful place talking about the changes we had noticed. A weight had been lifted from the relationship. A new, 'magical' but calming, centring presence is amongst us. It feels as if we have created a bond, a family, even though at present there are only two of us, and we have a responsibility to that family. It is fun, it is exciting, and it is a challenge. We are both survivors, and have been through major ordeals in our lives so far. Being able actively to give commitment to something so important as another loving human being is wonderful.

Although there are married Friends at Young Friends General Meeting, most Young Friends seem to leave YFGM when they get married. Sometimes these things just happen at the same time. But it feels as if getting married is a slightly unacceptable thing to do, as if marriage is outdated and wrong. This is true for many Young Friends, and it is hard to stand up and say 'I believe in the sanctity of the life-long commitment of marriage'. It is a daunting thing to say when you feel out of place. I talked to a friend of mine who recently got married, and the decision to marry seemed directly to affect her decision to leave YFGM.

It seems that unless you are a very strong voice, it is hard to belong to Young Friends General Meeting if you are married. Having said that, Young Friends I have spoken to have been really positive and supportive of our decision. I have often been asked how we managed to make the decision. It has been good for me to go over it, it has confirmed in me that it is the right decision to make.

Without love, we are nothing... **P8**.

K Family

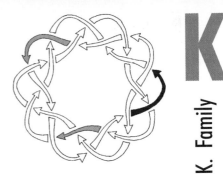

Family

We sometimes have a fear of:

losing our flexibility, choice, independence and identity.

Is this why some of us choose not to have children?
See **K7** *or* **K8**.

change.   *...in parental relationships,* **K2**.

revisiting past hurt and broken trust.   **K6**.

recreating negative patterns in relationships.   **J16**.

failure.   **K3**.

attachment, stagnation and a suffocating clinging.   **K5**.

no return.   **K10**.

K Family

K1   The myth of eternity runs through our whole lives, starting in childhood when we rely upon a sense of eternal stability and reliability, when we are given a sanitised reality, protected from the real world. When this is shattered, particularly when our parents split up or die, this security can be shattered, which can affect us deeply. The requirement in weddings to commit for life has been a major stumbling block for Young Friends' acceptance of the tradition. On the one hand, during a wedding we may say with all sincerity that we will love forever and mean it at the time, but on the other, this is something we can never know and which is beyond our control. It may be unfairly tempting fate and raises the spectre of failure for those who face grave difficulties in keeping their promise.

Is this how you view marriage? **J18** *expresses a different view.*

K2   When I was a child I put my mum on a pedestal. She was always strong, always loving, always there for me. She and my dad were the perfect couple, happily married, loving, supportive of each other and of me.

As I grew up this picture began to change. This was sometimes a shock. It changed because Mum recognised that I was becoming an adult and began to treat me as an equal. She began to show me a fuller picture of herself and her relationships with others. This happened in stages; I suppose she monitored how much I could deal with at a time.

I remember the first time I found out that my parents' marriage had not always been easy. I had always known that they are very different people. Mum is very passionate, emotional and creative. Dad is steady and rational. In many ways they complement each other, but sometimes she has fallen in love with someone who mirrors her creative side. It was a shock to me to find out that there had been affairs, but I also found out just how solid my parents' marriage is and how they have managed to deal with this, however painful it was.

As I got older, Mum began to share more with me. There were

no big secrets to reveal, we just began to talk about her fears, her insecurities and the unhappiness of her childhood. I learnt of her strengths and her talents in a truer sense than when I had idealised her as the perfect mother. And so our relationship has grown. We have become more equal. We have become friends. I hope that now I can be of support to her as well as leaning on her as a source of strength to me. I no longer put her on a pedestal, but I love her for the complicated, imperfect person that she is.

We are lovers, friends, partners, children, parents,
sisters, brothers… **P9**.

K3 *The death of one who did not belong.*

I did not belong to him, though he thought that I did.
He did not belong to the culture he came from.
He did not belong to the culture he chose, though he thought he did.
He left his first family in search of himself.
He left his new family in search of fame, though he was not to find it.

He found many friends in the world who thought he was a genius.
His abandoned family thought he was malicious, an emotional black-mailer who made us feel guilty for loving the things he did.
His timing was impeccable, he played exquisitely.
His timing was impeccable, he knew when to hurt us most.
He rejected us in favour of music and friends.
He rejected us by leaving us, guilt-tripping us and finally by dying, leaving us with the ultimate in rejection and emptiness.

K4 Our culture and our stories are forever changing. We face another world to that of our parents. But because it is different does not mean that it is harder. Change may be hard for many already adjusted to previous ways of doing things. Understanding the world requires flexibility.

K Family

It is often said that there is less commitment in our world than there has been. People are cut off from their society and their family, unwilling to commit to relationships or to career. There is an element of truth to this. Commitment has recently been having a bad press, and images of commitment in the media are increasingly linked to pain, suffering and sacrifice. Our society is increasingly based upon choice and personal freedom, at least in its ideology. There's not much freedom for the homeless and dispossessed! But the loss of commitment is not all negative.

In past times, the classic model of relationships has involved a wife dependent upon her husband-provider. Everything about the woman was associated with nurture and dependency, while the man was seen as independent and strong in himself. Such stereotypes have changed greatly, but there are strong residual perceptions around that even the most progressive can hold.

The Religious Society of Friends is constantly changing too... see **B10**.

Can we cope with changes to our communities? Try **L16**.

K5 Does my belonging to a family imply their ownership of me? In a human sense, does belonging equate to ownership? Being in a family does mean that you own many things (reputation, upbringing, ancestors) which are hard to disown.

K6 We had some fun times in my family. We used to go to the beach all the time, and my parents played with us – they even pretended to eat mud pies and things.

We used to talk to each other; we'd all be sitting in the bed cuddled up and we'd talk about everything and nothing – that's what it was like.

When I was six, my brother and I were in bed and he held me down and molested me. I went to my mum straight away, crying and I told her what had happened. My mum said I was lucky to have a brother. She said to learn about these things, because she didn't have a brother and she was innocent when she was a child. I couldn't understand what she meant. I didn't keep it a secret, but no-one listened to me. It was like running round in circles and hitting your head against a brick wall. A dinner lady said 'Tell your mum, that's a family thing'.

Looking back, I can see my mum couldn't cope. She let my brother abuse me for ten years and another man abuse me for six years; she blamed me for it. I don't think she really knew what she was taking on when she had children.

We used to go to Meeting for Worship most weeks. I wasn't thought of much as an individual at meeting, but it was a peaceful place, somewhere I could spend time with other families who were just 'normal'. Young Friends General Meeting makes me feel connected with my Quaker roots.

In some ways I feel that I've got such different experiences to everyone else, that I'm not the same as them, and I want to go home, because it feels familiar, but I don't. I don't think I'd fit in there anyway – I've changed now.

Childline – 0800 1111.

K7 'Why do you want to have children?'

I asked my partner this, some time ago, when we were discussing our future. He was stumped. It had never occurred to him that there was an alternative. Just because I don't want to have children of my own does not mean I don't like them, but the only way I can imagine being a parent is by an accident caused by contraception failure. The idea of a couple deciding to try to have children sounds to me like the ultimate commitment.

It hit me during a Meeting for Worship, the enormity of this decision. Once you are a parent your whole life changes and nothing is ever the same again. The sacrifices are huge, and I can't imagine wanting to exchange my gregarious and girlie (tarty?) life for a parental one with fewer holidays, less time to myself and someone else to think of before myself. Because these are the things I watched my mother go through having the three of us.

When people ask me why I don't want children, I generally give two answers:

1. I can't stand pain, and the idea of childbirth fills me with nausea and revulsion.
2. I don't want to bring up children on my own, and I don't trust that the father would hang around to help with child-care. Besides, I may not want him to be part of my life, even if he should be part of theirs.

Children are the ultimate commitment in a relationship, not marriage. I was brought up by my mother who was a single parent for most of my childhood. I do not believe this makes the child disadvantaged. I believe I am a fairly together woman. I have lapses of complete insanity; but everyone has those, not just children of single parent families. I don't want to bring up a child alone because I saw how hard it was for my mother. And there are, of course, a host of other issues. If one child is more gifted than the others in one field, how do you balance the attention you give to them all? If one has special needs of some sort, what of those that don't?

Although I am a reasonably strong woman, I don't believe I am strong enough for the weight that being a parent carries, and as such, I don't believe I could do the best for my children. If I had confidence in my relationship with my male partner, that he was going to be part of the support for the child, then my feelings would be different. But the doubt is always there. The man can always abandon the mother and child. And often they do.

My partner's answer was: 'I know a lot of people who have had children, and from what they say, I will be missing out on part of life if I don't have them too... '. I felt this was no reason to have children and told him so in no uncertain terms. He was hurt because I had considered this issue and come to a decision after some careful contemplation, something unusual as he was the one in our relationship that tended to act logically whereas I tend to act on gut reaction.

K8 Having children scares me. I wonder if I am too selfish to devote my life to another being, to be ruled by someone else's selfish needs and desires. Then I wonder if in fact motherhood could be the most incredible, selfless loving experience of my life. I wonder how my relationship expectations fit round the responsibilities of having children, which are more lifelong than I want my relationships to be.

The writer of **M2** *is scared too, of being tied down.*

K9 Through getting to know my two nieces I have begun to break down some of my fears of having children. Children need to be treated, like any other person, with respect. They need to be treated as equals, but allowances have to be made for the fact that, as children, they may not have the experiences or the language to understand things and express themselves in the same way as adults. They are not a different breed; I was wrong to lump them together by saying I don't like children. My friends pointed out to me that all the children I spent time with enriched me and that I enriched their lives. More than that, I enjoyed their company.

Living near to my two nieces has been one of the most wonderful experiences of my life. I have seen them grow over three and a half years and watched them change. The eldest and I have deep conversations and we share our thoughts. We discuss racism, death, divorce, God, anything that comes up. I am totally honest with her. If she asks me something that I don't feel able to answer, I tell her. She knows I don't have all the answers. If I feel uncomfortable with her questions, I tell her. I hope that I am honest in my answers. When talking about God and Jesus, I tell her that some people believe this, and some people believe that, and I believe this. And all these beliefs are equally valid.

At my father's funeral, my eldest niece was six and I was 22. My overriding memory is of her holding my hand and letting me cry, and comforting me more than anyone else. As soon as I was able, I told her how much support she gave me. Like adults, children need reassurance that they are doing the right thing.

We struggle and celebrate... **P9**.

K10 My cousin's death was sudden, violent and tragic. It sent shock-waves through my family, radically altering our lives. I gained a profound knowledge of just how utterly precious my family is to me. At that time, my sense of belonging to a group was stronger than anything I had experienced before. I prayed: Please God, Please Don't Let Anybody Else Die.

When my mother was diagnosed with cancer, I committed myself wholeheartedly to our relationship, with an urgency that overwhelmed me. During the one and a half years of her illness, I increasingly devoted more and more time to my family. They became my community. My primary relationship. My life.

In the last few weeks before my mum died, we gathered. To care for her, to be with her and to be with each other. In the final days, none of us went more than ten seconds away from her bedside. For me, every moment was a resonant communion. Each hour seemed to bring a new permutation of agony, love, confusion, torture, beauty and grace.

After the funeral, when it was all over, I returned to my college and my friends. I was desolate without my family. I wanted desperately to be with the people who knew me and knew what I had been through.

I have no map for my grief. Now, seven months after my mother's death, I understand very little of what is happening to me. I don't think I will ever comprehend the enormity of the impact it has had on my life. But I do see myself growing, my ideas evolving. I am searching out my identities – as a young woman with talents and passions, as a frightened daughter who has lost her mum.

With the shocking realities of birth and death, families are inevitably organic. I know that my family group will continue to shift and change, for change is life. I know also that whoever and wherever we are, we will share much of the joy and the pain that is yet to come.

Cruse (Bereavement) – 0181 332 7227.

L   Community

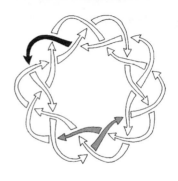

Community

What makes Young Friends different from other groups of people?

Solidarity. *All groups can give this... see* **L2**.

Being part of a minority. *Does this mean we rely on labels?* **L3**.

Being with good friends who have enough respect and love to just let me be. *Try looking through section* **D. Young Friends**.

It can be a bit defensive and insular.

Must you believe the 'right thing' in order to belong? **L6**.

We differ from other groups of young people in the variety of people, experiences and beliefs among Young Friends, in the discussions, the depth, the way we organise things, and the events themselves. *See* **D2**.

L   Community

L1   I feel that the most important truth we can learn from the life of Jesus is that we all belong to one community, one family from whom no one is excluded, a commonwealth that all people share in. This is a very difficult commitment to live up to if we take it as anything more than a vague platitude expressing general equality. How can we belong in any meaningful way to something so large as everybody? In practice this can be easier than it sounds, as individually we meet a limited number of people in our lives. However, international trade and the mass media connect us more and more to the international family to which we belong. This belonging commits us to loving all people and acting out that love in our lives. Central to this is our commitment to truth.

> *Do you achieve unity between your personal, social, political and spiritual responsibilities? Read* **N1***.*

L2   Groups help us overcome our insecurity and empower us. They enable us to gather with like-minded sisters and brothers in a common purpose, and help to express identity. There is a danger, though, that such expression can be mistaken for the identity itself, and thus we come to limit ourselves. Friends have to be aware of this problem, particularly when asking members and attenders to take on further responsibilities.

L3   When people are committed or attached to a group, they all too often get classified as a permanent, stereotypical part of that group. This labelling or categorisation is restrictive – it shows people in a prejudiced light, in which others tend to see only certain, expected, sides of their character and not appreciate the person as a whole or see their real, whole potential. I'm probably guilty of that as much as anyone, but I try to see people as people, rather than as 'hippies' or 'gays' or 'lecturers' or whatever. The other side of commitment is that when you commit yourself to people you get commitment back. If you are part of a group, that group will generally support you and you will start to belong.

Does commitment come before belonging? **P2**.

L4 Paradoxes of belonging keep groups moving. If it were possible to have a group of people who were of like mind on everything, so that individual commitments merged perfectly with what belonging to the group required, that group would never be able to move beyond itself. It would be paralysed by its lack of difference. We often talk about groups (notably the Religious Society of Friends) which are able to incorporate a wide range of views and experiences, blending different voices in harmony. Perhaps more important is that dissonances demand resolutions which move the music onward…

L5 Do you feel part of a group? In youth culture people wear their identities as part of a group on their sleeves, quite literally. I went to a rave shop once but didn't feel enough of a 'proper rave' to buy the cool T-shirts! My brother didn't feel like a real rocker or Goth because he had a normal job, but a lot of those wearing all the Goth gear had desk jobs and wore suits all week!

Labels as identities… **J13**.

L6 We decide whether we belong, but also others can (on purpose or by mistake) exclude people who do not easily fit in, even if they are committed. I used to regularly attend the Christian Union at polytechnic and play violin in the music group, but I never felt at the centre of it all because I believed the wrong things. In any group there is a core of requirements that make people belong. Commitment to anything else not entirely consistent with this will prevent your easy belonging to a group.

J18 shows how a commitment to something as conventional as marriage can exclude you.

L   Community

L7   Commitment does not necessarily imply exclusivity. Exclusivity, or not, is something that must be talked about, and boundaries must be set depending on the individuals concerned and what suits them.

Exclusivity is not necessarily negative… see **J14**.

L8   My lifestyle is a matter of giving and taking, responsibility and challenge. I also want to belong to the whole school team. Because this is the first class I am teaching in primary school, a lot of things are coming towards me. Because of the feeling of commitment and belonging, I can cope with all of it. If I didn't feel committed, I would only be willing to do half of what I am doing now (I think).

L9   I have ideas about changing things in a very real way. I think of myself as a 'career person', but not in a 'high-powered business executive' kind of way. I have ideas about changing the world by talking to people and doing things on a very personal level. People often say to me, 'Why don't you want to get into films?' My answer is that films don't work on a personal level. It concerns me the amount of damage that Margaret Thatcher and too many years of Tory rule have done by making everyone think about themselves.

Does it feel like this to you?

Do we only think about ourselves?

L10   Once you get into helping other people and talking about issues that do affect you, such as poverty, the environment etc., you can get stimulated. While you are helping other people, you get a lot of self-satisfaction into the bargain: you start to appreciate yourself for what you are and tend to get a completely different perspective on life.

A lot of people have got into a rut — there's nothing for me, I don't have any money or a job, etc. — but if everyone started to rediscover the joy of helping each other, they would realise that there is so much to live for. People tend to get too focused in on themselves.

A lot of people really believe that money is the answer to everything. They get conned into the get-rich-quick idea that is promoted by the National Lottery, and they say, 'when I have lots of money everything will be all right'. It upsets me so much to think that they just don't see it – they'll never get loads of money, and you only have to look at the selfish, rich bastards in power to realise that having lots of money doesn't make anything better, it just turns people into selfishly arrogant, bloody-minded assholes.

Look to section **N. Lifestyle and Responsibility** for expansion of this theme.

L11 Commitment can be powerful and real without a sense of belonging, particularly for younger Friends unconnected to a particular place or lifestyle. I am involved in social and community work where I live, and feel comfortable yet do not belong. This can give me a distance and an objective viewpoint.

L12 In modern life, belonging to local communities is complex. A child could be born in Newcastle, live there for thirteen years, then move to Gloucester. In the new place he is made to feel unwanted and out of place. After fifteen years, people in Gloucester accept him (not that it took that long to be accepted), but the 28 year old now feels he belongs wherever he is and that nobody should demand that somebody belongs somewhere.

L13 Why was it that miners cared so much about the mines in their communities being shut down in the early 1980s? You would think they would be glad not to do a dark, dangerous, exhausting, boring job all day and die early of lung disease. But it was the wrenching apart of their communities that hurt so much and drove them to fight the closures. The miners had developed solidarity in their working groups even before they started campaigning on the closures. That solidarity was essential for actually working the pits themselves, as well as for defending their existence in the struggle. It might have been more helpful if they had been offered alternative work together as a group instead of piecemeal retraining: their self-respect was wrapped up in their work. A similar problem faces all of Britain's millions of unemployed people. So many already had commitments such as children and mortgages when they became unemployed.

L14 There is often a difference between the fact of belonging to something and the subjective feeling of a sense of belonging. I belong to the country of my birth and always will, but my sense of belonging to this country may vary in strength.

L15 Spending a year living and working in a very different culture immediately after leaving school taught me what it can be like 'not to belong'; but it was interesting to watch the different ways in which the group of young people in the same situation coped with it. There were those who took the decision not to belong or assimilate more than was absolutely necessary to a society that was so far removed from the one that they knew, loved and valued; and there were those who, like me, felt we had no choice but to find a way of 'belonging' there. I found it through my work, and realised I could in a sense 'belong' anywhere I had a role to fill, even if that role was the slightly ambiguous one of the 'foreign' (always foreign) teacher. I also realised then how important to me the idea that every person is 'unique, precious and a child of God' had become. It helped to break down gradually the feeling of being unable to 'belong' anywhere among people whose world-view was so different from my own. If I wanted to resuscitate a worked-to-death George Fox quote, I'd say that in my experience, if we are committed to answering that of God in everyone, we tend to find it; and if we walk cheerfully in that commitment, perhaps we can find the places we belong, anywhere in the world.

For another look at deciding not to belong see **C4**.

L16 In Britain we have more in common with other European cultures in terms of our connectedness with locality than with young societies such as the United States, which are characterised by their transience. Some sense of continuity is provided by old buildings, mature surroundings, which give a sense of belonging to a place. Modern societies are highly individualistic. The concept of freedom leads to hedonism and selfishness and the death of communities in the old sense.

We should strive to build new communities in which the individual is respected and we are prepared to accommodate each other's perspectives and needs. We all feel the loss of community, but there is no point in trying to return to a pre-modern community. Traditions are important and provide a sense of rootedness and stability, but in insecure communities that feel under threat they can be used for fascist purposes. The question that faces us now is: how do we now build strong multi-racial communities that are not exclusive and respect difference? In Britain, we may be proud of our tradition of tolerance and integration. You find an incredible number of places of worship of different religions close to each other. We have a tradition of cosmopolitanism, and foreign cultures are incorporated into everyday life; the Indian curry, for example. Yet our Quaker Meeting, in the middle of an inner city area, seems to have invisible barriers that prevent working class people from getting involved. We define ourselves as open-minded, but is this to comfort ourselves rather than a reflection of reality?

All political parties talk of the necessity of community, but there seems little political will to provide the necessary funding. The growth in the divide between rich and poor has had a profound effect on the community. New possibilities for the better off, such as the Internet and world-wide travel, have encouraged communication and helped to increase understanding between communities. But they have also made life for people on a subsistence income all the more frustrating.

Problems with disunity and alienation from our meetings... **C9**.

Churches within the wider community... **C8**.

L   Community

L17 Patriotism is about belonging to and having a strong commitment to your country or nation. It is a bad thing because it leads to war. Strong commitment to one group excludes those committed to another. It would be better to commit yourself to principles, such as education for all or not allowing anyone to starve, and start by fostering those principles in your own country.

L18 It is no good trying to make the European nations unite until the people feel European – until they feel they belong in the same box. How can you want to have political decisions affecting you made partly by shadowy figures across the sea who you don't really know anything about? A truly united Europe will only come about if and when people in different nations come to know each other ('in the Spirit') and appreciate from the heart each other's rights and needs for consideration. The process has begun well, with school exchanges, town twinning, the opening of internal borders and other such sensible steps. Media coverage is better than nothing, but it is too easily taken as fiction – there's no substitute for actually getting to know the people. When the ordinary people in Europe come to trust those from other nations as much as they trust people from their own, that will be the time for union. Forced commitment is weak (look at the Irish and the Scots!). The only long-lasting commitment will be the one that arises naturally out of our feeling of belonging together.

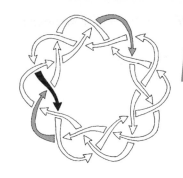

Power and Powerlessness

How does your spiritual path affect your commitments?

I am committed to thinking about and exploring my spirituality over time, by thinking in my everyday life about my reasons and motives for doing things and about the deeper beliefs and values that guide me, which I sometimes feel make me different from the 'ordinary' (secular) socially conscious individual.

> **M14** talks of the importance of a sense of idealism and purpose.

Choices to commit are inevitably influenced by our existing commitments…

> Our time and energy are finite… **M9**.

My spiritual path is exciting, difficult, challenging and gets ever more interesting and changeable.

> For a different view, see **M10**.

M   Power and Powerlessness

M1   As an individual free spirit, I know it's often hard to find a sense of direction strong enough to push myself in, even temporarily. Do we collectively need some short-term commitments? Commitments don't have to be permanent (I realised that myself recently) or set in stone. They don't have to dominate everything. Our freedom is a wonderful thing; it gives us so much scope. But freedom is pretty pointless if you never go anywhere. Perhaps we need an overall sense of direction, to say 'we're doing something!'.

M2   I'm really scared of being tied down, committed. From my position on (I feel) the edge of society, a 'proper' job, being tethered to one place for five days of every week, having to be in the same place, doing the same stuff, looks like chains. I'm often telling myself that I've got to grow up and accept the way the world is, but the prospect is awful. I feel it wouldn't be as bad if I had some idea of a vocation, but there is so much in the world that offends my (perhaps unduly high) principles, it would seem like the beginning of the slippery slope if I said, 'oh, well, it's only a little bit of exploitation, pollution, excessive waste that goes on here; that's OK'.

It's not as if it's possible to get jobs doing interesting, creative, life-enhancing things. I could stack shelves at a supermarket (supporting a desperately exploitative industry), wait at tables in restaurants (serving meat), work behind a bar (serving alcohol), join the police force (if they'd have me since I have a hole in my nose – and learn how to beat up and torture my former friends), become a security guard on a construction site (helping destroy the environment even further), sell things like kitchens and double-glazing by telephone (promising credit, to people who can't afford and don't want them). What options do I have?

M3   Having few long-term commitments in work or relationships means I pass through many places and situations. It is sometimes hard to live with the knowledge that I have the chance, the freedom, to move on when others don't. I can go to help out in a day centre for mentally ill people for a few days, and do my best for the patients and staff while I'm there, and learn a little about the problems they all face; but then I can leave. In fact I have to leave, and leave them with the problems. Having a period of freedom in my life like this is an opportunity I'm very grateful for, but not being able to commit myself to people or places can in itself bring pain. It would make the free life easier if I could adopt an attitude of detachment more often; but it would also destroy everything valuable about life.

The writer of **G7** *has a different approach to freedom.*

M4 All of us who throw our minds towards a more just and equitable world feel discouraged at times, that we're fighting against a tide, we're hopeless dreamers, we ought just to accept the way the world is. I hold in my mind a proverb that goes something like 'she is a fool who does nothing because she could only do a little' – that and a gritty determination to *make a difference.*

N21 questions how others' priorities affect our belonging and commitment.

M5 It is incredibly important to have a sense of purpose and idealism in life, as well as being pragmatic about it. Ideals and hope are essential to us. Our ideals go a long way to defining our identity as individuals. But often it is difficult to express in a meaningful way what those ideals are. It is all very well talking of truth, justice, equality, reason, consistency and integrity, or of tenderness, mercy, compassion or faith but if these words are to have meaning it is in their application. The challenge is in the expression. Our ideals, along with our identity, are a shifting ground, making it more difficult and challenging to maintain a clear sense of purpose over time. We often find it easier to say what we are not committed to or what is incompatible with our ideals. Hierarchies were high on the hit list, as were many modern-day ideologies (well described by Jonathan Dale in his Swarthmore

Lecture), which lead to self-centredness in the battle to survive, a lack of security or foundations, and despair on a grand scale. There is a fear of vulnerability, which extinguishes our humanity.

M6   In the commitments I make, I voluntarily restrict the freedom of my future self. I could always break them… but then what's the point of making them?

M7   A friend told me once that he never felt as if he belonged in the area where he grew up; he thought this was because his family never got involved in the life of that area. Feeling one belongs seems only to come about through involvement; and involvement requires commitment. The Oxford English Dictionary tells us that commitment is an undertaking or pledge that restricts freedom of action, a dedication to or involvement with a particular doctrine, course of action etc. Dedication to a person could take the place of doctrine or course of action here. Sometimes this might restrict freedom of action: you've said you'll be somewhere so you can't go somewhere else, or you'll go to see a friend who is ill, for example, instead of doing something that would perhaps be more fun (depending on the friend and the state they are in). So, on the surface at least, commitment is quintessentially about restriction of choice.

M8   My commitment to living in the Spirit, the same one that infused early Friends, leads me to an adventuresome life. It is so exciting to address letters to faceless bureaucrats 'Dear Friend' instead of 'Sir/Madam', thus trying to recognise that it's not just a machine who deals with my letter.

M9   Commitment takes time and energy. Like everyone I have finite resources of time and energy. This means that the number of commitments I can honour is limited. As I see it, time and energy spent with Young Friends nationally means less spent with your local meeting, and the more actively committed you are to, say, campaigning for disarmament, the less actively committed you can be to your family (for example).

I can believe in huge numbers of things at once, but I cannot commit myself to action on all my beliefs at the same time and keep that commitment.

M10 I'm a fairly apathetic bloke. In fact, compared to the image of the 'ideal' Quaker – so committed, so energetic, so peaceful, simple, respectful, so demoralising... – I'm extremely apathetic.

It's not easy to stay convinced of the urgency, or even the possibility, of changing the world. Personally I could never become obsessed by one issue, because I always start thinking of another issue that deserves my concern, or of the way in which all the problems are interlinked. Being concerned about everything gives one a sense of disempowerment.

So what unites us as Quakers? Section **E** *or* **P4**.

M11 There's nothing beyond self-interest here. In fact, there isn't even any reason why you're alive. Blind chance, that's all. It could just as easily have been a different sperm all those years ago and you would never have existed at all. So if there's no meaning, what's the point? Why not just sit back, relax and spend the rest of your life in a semi-vegetative state in front of the TV?

And besides that, of course, whatever you do, you're bound to be wasting your time. No matter what your cause, no matter how hard you work, you could have done better. You could have been more useful somewhere else. The world is such a big place and there's so much that needs fixing, it's impossible to find the most efficient way to use your time. Forget it. If you can't fix it – and let's face it, enough people have tried – don't bother.

Forget that middle-class guilt. Just because you're comfortable and so many people aren't, it doesn't follow that you should feel bad about it. Be thankful for what you have, and try not to let your social conditioning get you down.

M12 My uncertainty about the future limits my ability to make commitments, and creates great uncertainty about where to direct my energy.

M13 Commitment is something I'm personally very bad at. For years, possibly my whole life, I've lived on the edge of things, seldom or never devoting my entire energy to anything, and never for very long. I have had minor, weak commitments – maybe a better word is 'attachments' – and I have had moments of enthusiasm and inspiration when I've jumped into something with both feet and been seriously involved – for a short time. I've always liked the idea of being free, not tied down to anything, able to get up and move on whenever I wanted. Commitments feel threatening in a way because they are a tie to a particular group of people.

M14 Modern societies are highly individualistic. Individuals are valued above all else. The concept of freedom can lead to hedonism and selfishness and the death of communities in the old sense.

M15 If I decide I'm going to be a campaigner against homelessness, does that mean I miss an opportunity that arises much nearer to me and is more suited to my abilities to, for example, become involved in work with elderly people? In practice I do bits of everything, and when I stop to think, wish I could do more of everything.

Try **N13**.

To social action.

Social action comes in different forms... **N16**.

To environmental/political/social issues that are limited, as in the Real World Coalition.

N9 *looks at some of these issues, as does* **N20**.

To simplicity.   **N2**.

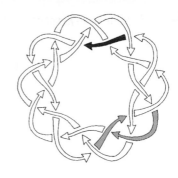

Lifestyle and Responsibility

As a Young Friend, what issues should you be most committed to?

To what the inner voice instructs me. To being true. To expression of faith. To loving and creating.

> **N28** *shows how important it is to be yourself.*

To following the will of God or (for non-believing Quakers) doing the most good.

> *Doing the most good at work…* **N17**.

To equality in all aspects of life: fair trade, freedom (of speech, movement etc.)

> **N15** *looks at how this affects everyday life.*

To peace.
> *The peace testimony is still alive and well within Young Friends…* **N13**.

N Lifestyle and Responsibility

N1 Perhaps the most important thing in my life is to try to achieve a unity between the personal, social, political and spiritual responsibilities I have assumed and my corresponding intuitive commitments. I feel out of touch, unconnected, distant from God when I find myself with responsibilities I do not believe in. I have promised myself to remain in any job only as long as I believe in that job and would do it without pay or in spite of inconvenience. The moment my heart is not in my social responsibilities, I try to reduce them and shift my burden into areas for which I feel passionate commitment.

Commitment in work... see **N25**.

N2 How far is far enough? Should we feel virtuous for being vegetarian or guilty for not being vegan? Is it good to trade in a BMW for a mini, or should we be cycling to the station? Such questions arise continuously, yet there can be no straightforward answer. A testimony must be a way of behaving, not a set of rules or ethics.

As a Young Friend beginning to evolve my own lifestyle, I have spent time considering how simple I wish that lifestyle to be. I am often appalled by the extravagance and complexity of the world around me, including the amount there is in my own life. Countering it at the current time involves swimming very much against the tide, and I have not always felt able to take up the challenge. I avoid the self-evidently excessive, but have then used that as a justification for much else that is not strictly necessary.

I feel uncomfortable with my own lifestyle because it does not reflect the simplicity that I can recognise and respect in others. However, I have come to realise that my attempts to commit to an outward simplicity are not the solution. I have also become more critical of the careless judgements of myself and others. I feel it is too easy for us to assume that the simpler lives are the better, applying bare rules to a more complex issue.

Simplicity is too easily interpreted as the opposite of complexity. Yet this view is suggestive of naïvety and innocence, which I do not believe to be implied. I am not aiming to achieve the simplicity of a child, which, however beguiling, I see as inadequate. Simplicity, rather, is awareness of the depth and complexity in which all of our lives are embedded, while retaining a sense of clarity. As such it is an inner, not an outer, objective.

N3 I have decided to buy a house in order to seek simplicity. So far, the process is far from simple – dealing with many companies, all so commercial. But living alone in a flat has felt so 'me-centred', and I feel the need to share an environment and my life with others. And making a friendly home will involve much commerce: furniture, cushions, bookshelves and all the cosy tastes, smells and sights I want to share. I hope God will guide me as I make each decision about spending the resources available to me.

Seeking God's guidance in daily decisions... **F15**.

N4 I sometimes think that I should spend as little as possible and give money to charity. But without some kind of commerce, in our world as it is, we would find living very hard. We need to learn to be more aware of how our choices complicate the lives of others. Maybe our choices should centre on the consequences of what we spend for those that produce and sell things to us. Buying plastic packed microwave meals 'for one' causes more human and animal suffering and pollution than buying vegetables from the corner shop and making a huge vat of curry.

N5 Can one really think globally without being antisocial locally? One should be conscious of how one affects the broader world *because* one wants to be polite to those around us, not despite that fact. Our desire to change the world beyond our immediate environment is an *extension* of the love that makes us desire to get on with people, and is not in opposition to it.

N6   The Religious Society of Friends has maintained a testimony to simplicity since its formation, which is still in evidence today. It is clearly manifest in the style of a Meeting for Worship, but also in our wider lives – perhaps in manner, in actions or in lifestyle. Yet it seems that achieving this simplicity can be something we find a struggle. There are many difficulties, especially in a world with so much inequality: almost any lifestyle in Britain will not match the simplicity enforced elsewhere.

Are the testimonies what unites us? **J2** or **P6**.

N7   I am left with great admiration for people who dedicate their lives to friendship: those following a career in care or medicine, those prepared to be arrested to prevent another road slicing through the countryside, or simply drivers who slow down to let me cross the road. My own commitment to social justice is an expression of this friendship and is also an attempt to encourage it. I do not wish to force my own beliefs and standards onto anyone else, but neither do I wish to cut them off from a better society, as our largely negative, stressful and unjust world threatens to do. I am committed to a world that nurtures friendship, instead of holding it back.

Commitment to friendship as an ideology… see **J4**.

N8   I really want to Lead By Example. But for this, humility is paramount. An arrogant approach achieves nothing and can put people off so much that it has the opposite effect. In trying to achieve a more harmonious world it is possible to create local disharmony, annoying people and causing tensions that negate the overall objective. I don't like the arrogance connected with telling people how they should live, on the basis that I know better. But after years of irritating people with my moralising and being constantly criticised for it, perhaps I have now swung too far the other way. It is nice to hold an idealised notion of myself humbly and meekly leading by example (not that I do), but it would hardly occur to my peers to start boycotting Nestlé after they notice me not using Nestlé products.

If I am completely honest with myself, my avoiding preaching to people because of the arrogance associated with it is in some ways partly to justify my laziness and lack of energy. It is so hard to continue to be fired up about an issue five years on. All the apathy and disinterest I meet with makes it more difficult to find the confidence and enthusiasm to talk to people about what matters to me. I am a coward in that I want to avoid annoying people and causing tensions, although I know from my own experience that I am often hostile and defensive to people who moralise at me, because I know they are right, yet I may still change my habits later as a result of it.

As the millennium approaches, we in the technologically advanced countries are enjoying high standards of living at the expense of millions of other people who do not have enough to eat. We hardly have time to ponder such facts in our fast-track lifestyles and societies. We have created a time-bomb and the certainty that unless we transform our values, priorities and behaviour, future generations will not be here to see in the next millennium. Our technological development far outweighs our spiritual maturity.

See **B6**.

N9 I am a member of my monthly meeting and have lived in this city for ten years. I am a Green Party city councillor, and warden of the Friends Meeting House. Amongst other things, I have a commitment to: my city, to the world as a planet, and to playing my part in making both a better and more fulfilling place to live in; to my meeting, and accepting burdens and duties in my capacities as a warden and as a member; to Friends in Britain Yearly Meeting, with many of whom I find I share passion and similar commitments; to my family, with whom I share many experiences, past and present; to my friends, and my sexual partner, with whom I share a love that has many inexplicable dimensions.

These statements are true, and I am unashamed of them. A danger, though, is that I start to define myself in terms of these commitments and my responses to them. Another is that I start to revere the secondary 'tools' that further my more fundamental aims. I plead guilty to reverence of the Religious Society of Friends, though the danger is much greater with my commitment to the Green Party. Like any other social organisation, the Religious Society of Friends is an artificial construction designed to suit the needs of those that come in contact with it. It may be effective and provide essential support, but commitment to the values, beliefs, witness and aspirations of the Society is (or should be) deeper than that to the Society itself.

What is the source of my deepest commitments? Why is that such a difficult question? Because life is not one-dimensional in its essence. My passions, my faith and my commitments inform one another, arising as they do out of my culture and my truth. They are mysterious and impelling. Is it not true to say that for Friends the essence of our faith lies in our experience? And that such experience is a many-coloured patchwork of emotions, stimuli and people, and that our responses also impact upon such experience? To say there is one source (be that 'faith' in 'God', 'truth' or whatever) is to beg the question.

Authoritarian religions (those that locate religious authority in a book or in what other people tell us) stand accused by me of encouraging their followers to duck their own human spiritual responsibilities, and can be downright dangerous. We see the danger of over-commitment to a single idea or institution all too often. At the same time, contentment can too often be expressed as complacency. Doubt plays a strong, positive role in our faith as Friends. Pity not those Friends who are on the point of resigning from the Society: those who take up the challenge and wrestle with their faith without crutches should be encouraged in their questioning.

It is often said that our system of belief, one based upon our own passions, experience, actions and culture, encourages liberal laxity. But this is to deny the essence of Quakerism and to misunderstand its consequences. Rather, to accept such a system of belief is to accept the full discipline of our duties, to God, to ourselves and to our fellow creatures. This is so much harder than the blind faith demanded by many other religions, but it is an essential part of the search for truth.

So my faith arises out of a complex web of interconnections. I believe in truth and justice; I experience love and believe in it (sometimes); I believe in the ethic of sustainability as well as having a number of other values with names that do not adequately convey their variety and complexity; I have passions whose source is magical and inexplicable. I am driven, by what I sometimes do not know, to act against injustice, deceit, selfishness, corruption, and institutionalised murder and insanity. But such actions inform my faith as well as being an expression of it. Indeed, they are an intrinsic part of my faith. It is no good my sitting there in silence expecting fully formed inspiration to hit me before acting upon my convictions. The separation between faith and action is a false distinction. I have a dynamic, ever changing, open relationship with my faith. That is how I learn.

Am I driven by guilt? We can too often mistake the guilt we feel with the commitment itself. Feelings of guilt come when I feel I am not adequately living out my commitments. But often guilt has been a sign of my having expectations that are impossible to meet, and has paralysed my action. I have learned to accept myself, to some extent to prioritise my commitments (though there is plenty of room for improvement!) and to live a faithful life with self-confidence.

N10 I have a problem with keeping too much of my 'action in the world' under the umbrella of the Religious Society of Friends. I often wonder why this is. Is it because Quakerism is about a way of life, and therefore anything that I do is done because I am committed to Quakerism and it doesn't need a label? Is it because I am unwilling to have everyone interpreting all my actions as consequences of the fact

I am a Quaker? I think it is partly about wanting to interact with a wider group of people and needing stimulation and challenge.

It would in many ways seem easier to do everything under the Quaker umbrella, but there would be a danger of becoming complacent and believing that the Society is the only organisation through which change should occur. I am very concerned that the Society does not become too insular in that respect and perhaps supports other organisations rather than setting up duplicate ones. On the other hand, however, I feel that there are occasions when it would be enormously helpful for the Society to come out with more corporate – or maybe even just strong, public, individual – statements about social, political, cultural, economic and environmental problems and, if possible, let these lead to action. But would this mean we were not practising what we preach?

E17 *talks of shared Quaker values.*

What do we share? P4.

N11 To me, there should be no division between sacred and secular. If Quakerism is to be a way of life, not a one-day-a-week religion, then when is there room for anything completely secular? Should we not be viewing everything as sacred in a way? Should not every situation we come across be approached in the same way that we approach traditionally spiritual/sacred issues? Is this not in fact what we have attempted through holding our business meetings as Meetings for Worship?

N12 Living in the developed, minority world, I am forever conscious of how difficult it is to lead a life without plastic. It is so hard to live sustainably here. I know that every day my existence is having a negative effect on the planet, as I cause the consumption and waste of energy and resources. I am therefore committed to making up for this, and more. I am determined to ensure that my life will have as much of a positive outcome for the earth as possible. Just to balance out the pollution I shall cause in my lifetime (however much I try to reduce it) will be enough of a challenge. I believe many of the high hopes I have for my lifestyle stem from my upbringing as a Quaker. I am proud of the values my ancestors had and the lives they led, and I do not want my own life to be a comparative disappointment.

So what do we actually do about this sort of conviction?
You could start reading about it from **N24**.

N13 The urgency of our task does not necessarily mean that we have to race around manically putting things right. We may find this to be counterproductive. Friends have developed various disciplines over the years which, relived in the spirit of love and peace from which they grew, could serve us well. We have sensed the mysterious power of silent waiting in Quaker worship. Many of us have glimpsed its potential for loving transformation if held in our hearts as we approach problems. It is in worship that we can let go of our unceasing thoughts and passions. We can move beyond the rational into the realm of the Spirit. The more we wait and grow in the stillness, the more we engage the creative Christ-spirit within and the more powerful our work for peace becomes, anchored as it is in the universal love.

The essence of this is not new. These are words from my own experience, which Quakers and many others have described in many different ways over the years. The point is not in the words, but in the experience of each of us rediscovering their source and making this a central part of our lives.

This involves both discipline and commitment. The seeds of love in ourselves and others need constant care and attention if they are to grow and become strong patterns of peace in a divided world. If we are to meet the challenge of the age to secure harmony on our planet, we have to work on ourselves and help each other. Prayer and worship keep us in touch with the Source within that feeds us. The building of community among Friends and others helps us to feel within the Oneness with each other. Pursued with tolerance and love, our example may 'start to transform world society into a true community' (M. Scott Peck).

In my work in Russia and in areas of conflict and war such as Chechnya over the last few years, I have often been face-to-face with overwhelming human suffering. I have been struck repeatedly by the meaninglessness of this violence and the loss it brings. The fragility of human beings has been brought home to me as I have seen death in its startling proximity and been reminded that each of us is only a breath away from death at any moment. At the same time as witnessing the destruction of war, I have been inspired by those close to it who have given their all to working for reconciliation. They have done this without the support of a peace movement or even the existence of role models in their societies for such kinds of activities. The peace movement in western countries can learn much from this work, carried out in conditions and danger difficult for us to contemplate.

The march for life and compassion from Moscow to Grozny in which Chechen women, Russian soldiers' mothers, Buddhist monks, Quakers and others took part came under the fire of Russian troops on several occasions. At one time, all 200 marchers were stopped at a Russian military checkpoint and surrounded by three rings of soldiers – one ring with fire-arms aimed at us. As dusk arrived and the rain poured down, the determination of the marchers and their vibrant spirit seemed only to grow. Conversations with the commander holding us there seemed to get nowhere – he expressed only scorn and disinterest. But the young soldiers we spoke to were deeply interested in who we were and why we were doing what we did. An 18 year old conscript summed up his opinion of the war: 'a disgrace for humanity'. The marchers, mainly women, seemed ready to stand fearlessly on that cold Chechen steppe for as long as it would take to stop the war. The statement of the march was read out several times:

Life is the greatest treasure on earth. Nobody can

deny a person's right to life. It is guaranteed by all national and international laws. The war in Chechnya has denied and continues to deny the right to life of thousands of people and deprives hundreds of people of their homes, property and happiness. The war must be stopped by any peaceful means.

I continue to work with many of those who took part in the march. Our activity is now based around rebuilding the society after the shattering effects of the war. The children are the most innocent victims – many are left wounded, without limbs or in a state of psychological trauma. Young people, women and others are keen to learn about the principles and methods of non-violent conflict resolution to help equip them in building lasting peace in their societies. Their work and enthusiasm gives me hope. If people from such differing cultures and societies can express such a sincere, brave and united call for peace in this situation, then the seeds of world peace can surely flourish elsewhere.

The task of peace does not demand of all of us that we walk into war zones calling for cease-fires. There is plenty of conflict, injustice and suffering in our home communities that must be addressed. Equally important is work to influence the power structures that govern our societies, in which corruption and self-interest are often the norm. Are we able to offer other, fairer examples and work for their implementation?

'Be patterns, be examples…' see **P8**.

N14 Young Friends from Russia, Chechnya and western Europe met in the North Caucasus republic of Adigeya in the summer of 1996. The proximity of the war in Chechnya informed much of our discussions on responding to conflict. The question was asked, 'what can we who live in places far away from armed conflict do?'. One response was that the way in which we live our lives, wherever we are, is the most important thing. If we respect and value one another and let an attitude of peace be apparent in our relationships and dealings, then we are already creating a more peaceful world. If we can learn to be conscious of our actions, words and Oneness, we are engaging in the task of peace.

N15 One of my ideals is that the whole of my life is worship, and I'll give an example of how I do this. I regard food and drink as sacramental (just as much as everything else), so I try to be aware of what I am doing to myself and others. I am vegan because I don't feel it necessary to cause pain and suffering to other beings. This helps me be a bit more aware of what I am putting into my body because most processed foods contain dairy products or meat, so I end up cooking for myself more and eating more wholefood – which leads to growing food, so getting more connected. Feeding myself (and others) with love and respect I find to be a really powerful well-being promoting process.

> Spirituality is difficult, if not impossible, to separate from lifestyle.
> You could compare this with **N4**.

N16 In my experience, commitment to action can enhance and express our spirituality. Every week, I visit an OAP with Parkinson's disease. I have committed myself to doing this for my three years at university. It can sometimes be difficult, but I feel our interaction and the opportunity for us both to be needed and useful enables the release of 'that of God' from within us.

It seems to me that in order to 'answer that of God' in everyone, it first has to be released. We need to be patterns and examples, committing ourselves to action. In doing so, we are creating conditions for the release of the divine from within everyone.

At the Young Friends' Jamboree, we considered what we were committed to in terms of social action and for what reason – our 'bottom line'. For me, it was all about releasing the divine. Through commitment to social action, 'that of God' is released both from those committed to working for change and from those they are working with. It is a twofold process: first, release as a result of inter-action and second, if inequality can be lessened, both at global and local levels, the divine has a further chance of release.

Releasing the divine... see **P7**.

N17 My awareness of the spiritual, you might call it God, has often come through my work. I spent a year working with children from the poorest areas of Belfast, and in the course of this work I found a deeper spirituality than I had experienced before. One moment in particular stands out in my mind, a 'Wow!' moment, through which I had a glimpse of the divine.

I was on the beach with a group of children. Some hadn't seen the sea before, and they rarely had the chance to experience the true freedom of childhood. Two brothers, Alan and John, were playing football in tracksuits and trainers. They were real hard Belfast lads, although they were both under ten. Where they were playing the sea had left pools of water in the sand. Every so often their ball would fly into one of these pools. At first they would carefully fish it out, but as they became more involved in their game they became less careful. Soon they were running in and out of the pools with a childlike delight that I had never seen in them before. Their faces were shining with joy. As I watched them play I knew I should have told them not to get their shoes and socks so wet, but I felt that something much too important was going on to worry about such trivial things. These boys were experiencing true freedom for the first time, and I felt privileged to witness it. It is through simple things such as the happiness of children that I feel a higher force at work in the world.

N18 I don't mean to say that 'Jesus was the son of God and died at the hands of Pontius Pilate and on the third day rose again', or even in a broader sense, 'Quakers are Christians'. I mean that Quakers all live out their faith – a faith in the spiritual impulse to act, the action releasing the divine, the divine releasing the action.

Living out our faith… go to **P. Living Testimony**.

N19 Outside the compound at Newbury,[1] we talk to the security guards, their first words echoing those of the soldiers to the woman participating in the vigil against cruise missiles at Greenham (*Quaker Faith & Practice*, 1995, 24.28). And when, instead of shouting at them as they have come to expect, we listen to them, engage, and sympathise with them, we begin to talk together about life, poverty, hope, they agree with us that this destruction is awful, unnecessary.

We know now, looking across the landscape where once was forest and that now looks like the moon, that we cannot stop this road, but maybe we can change people's minds about the necessity of roads, for the future, and then all the Government's billions won't be able to buy the help of these poor souls on the other side of the razor-wire.

They are caged in, or so it looks to us, with the hundreds of police and their vicious dogs and their riot gear like servants of a fascist state, and the pile drivers, three stories high, banging, banging. And we agree with them, Ruth and I, that it isn't fair that they, as security guards, don't merit ear defenders because they're not important enough, though they are just as near as the construction workers themselves.

Some have already left, jumped over, joined the protesters, and this one says he would if it weren't for his kids and the mortgage he's got with his partner. He and his mate here tell us we seem like ordinary people. We laugh. We *are* ordinary people, just like them. I feel happy that I'm doing the right thing, I'm in the right place, I'm helping the

---

[1] During the construction of a bypass around Newbury, there was a well publicised protest against the environmental effects of the mass road-building programme that was going on during the early 1990s. Some Quakers were involved in various similar protests at road-building sites around the country.

world just as much as if I had been down the other side of the route earlier and got inside the compound to hold up the construction.

B9 *speaks of 'doing the right thing' – in a different way!*

N20 Different people have different views on the environment. People faced with the same facts and knowledge will commit themselves to different things. This is because people are personally concerned about different aspects of the environment and are able to channel their commitment in different ways, depending on personal circumstances. The activist who D-locks himself to a bulldozer or sits in a tree to hamper road building and the person who tries to buy ethically and consume less are both acting out their beliefs in the way they feel happiest with. The level of action is right for them.

Does anyone else have the right to judge our commitment? Or the right to question us about it? I don't think anyone has the right to *judge* another person's commitment. However, I feel that someone does have the right to *question* another's commitment. What someone says and does can be different. Questioning someone can clarify the commitment for both parties. Something I have observed that we have in common as Quakers is a habit, a yearning, to question the ideals, motives, actions of ourselves and others.

N21 We often talk about what we would like or ought to be committed to. What is more important is to be aware of what we *are* committed to. Observe your behaviour! The suggestion that we *ought* to be committed can suggest that it is by someone else's judgement and values. A sense of belonging or desire to belong can put pressure on us to take on others' priorities.

There is a danger of falling into the trap described by Immanuel Kant: 'I sometimes suffer from the temptation to commit to things I do not enjoy, because of a sense of duty. The problem is that it is difficult to see what duty is, and I end up measuring it by what I do not want to do.'

On the other hand, choosing commitment can involve integrity, particularly when you choose a path you believe to be right rather than easy. If you learn a little of many languages, you will be able to communicate less than if you commit to learning one language well.

N22 If, in our everyday lives, we stop trying to make connections because Quakerism is a retreat of safety that we can fall back on, then we cease to be real.

N23 I often feel that whatever I could do would not make any revolutionary impact on the structure of society. But if changing the world is an ultimate and impossible goal, then changing a small part of it, my small part, is an attainable and satisfying step in the right direction.

*See **L9** for a different perspective.*

N24 I have always liked, and applied to myself as far as I could, Colossians 3:23 – 'Whatever you do, work at it with all your heart, as if it were for God... ' – *because it is for godde.*

I have rarely had a sense of the need to 'commit myself' intellectually or emotionally, in advance, before becoming involved in social action or campaigns of any sort; the same applies, in fact, to the various groups to which I am now in practice 'committed'. My feeling has usually been, especially in the broad area of 'social concern', that there is so much that I could be doing that an intellectual commitment to particular areas of concern above others is not helpful.

Commitment in everyday life often seems to mean simply a whole-hearted engagement in whatever the need of the moment is, in the faith that it will be of some use in the grand scheme of things.

N25 If you're in the right job, where you belong, and you are committed to it – it's what you believe in – you can be really happy. Work becomes a part of your identity, so it's important for it to be work you believe in.

More of our thoughts about work and vocation can be read in **B9**,
G7, D13, L9 *and* **M2**.

N26 Sustaining a belief that we are making a difference in the world
demands a shift in consciousness, from the muddy banks of life in a
dying society on a dead world into the live, fantastic, healing waters,
the fluid consciousness of true, right living. This is what Starhawk
names the 'power-from-within', and it embroils us in the constant
process, the Way which says 'there is no road to peace – peace is
the road'.

Taken from one of the modules at Woodbrooke, a particular
extract has stuck in my mind. [We] 'found ourselves without further
energy for the task of transformation. This changed when we shared
the following paragraphs from Julia Schofield Russell:

> As we transform ourselves, we transform the world. Not
> later. Now. Simultaneously. How can this be so? The
> practice of the politics of lifestyle springs from an under-
> standing of how things actually happen rather than the
> linear, cause-and-effect model. As we align ourselves with
> the regenerative powers of the Earth and the evolutionary
> thrust of our species, we tap into abilities beyond the
> ordinary. We move into the Tao.
>
> How do you initiate this process in your life?
> You can start just about anywhere. You can start with
> recycling, with your means of transportation, with your
> diet and food-buying practices, with composting, with
> your relationships, with meditation, tax resistance, right
> livelihood, housing, gardening, conservation, – it's up to
> you. What seems easiest, most obvious, or most urgent to
> you? Start there.

What we learned is that we had in fact already seriously begun the work – and play – of transformation, but each in a different way: through parenting, through politics, through spirituality, through an earth-conscious diet, through study. What we have in common is our motivation: our desire to heal the earth that we love.' (Rae, 1994)

N27 Our protestant background can lead us to a quest for absolute efficiency in our use of time, possessions, mind and body. I still feel this, but I wince at the sight of fast-food litter beginning its centuries-long decay in landfill tips. I think of nature's bounty: the leaf-litter strewn forest rides, bright sun, flavours and smells... wastefully poured forth whether we deign to sense them or not. Maybe it's a lesson to love what's there already before we waste and damage more: the sweet taste of water in preference to cola, local beauty over package tours, sunsets rather than soap operas...

N28 I find that the energy for transformation flows and ebbs in me, sometimes outwards to protest camps, letter-writing, public meetings and reading newspapers, and sometimes inwards to the space where I live. I get fed up with activists who don't respect each other, even those within their cause, not realising that they are perpetrating the system they oppose. I find that tidying my space, returning things I've borrowed, feeling and showing the love I have for the people around me, passing on what I don't need, thinking powerful, positive thoughts, eating without stuffing myself from fairly-traded or hand-grown, organic wholefoods, really does make a difference. However little my contribution, it seems to do something. I draw strength from knowing that by aligning myself with the powerful, living flow of Love, I am making a difference, changing the world by being myself.

Living Testimony

P1 Throughout our lives, we continue to ask the questions 'who are we?' and 'where do we come from?', and we watch the answers grow. Everyone forms their own identity in terms of what they are committed to, and what they belong to. It is through commitment and belonging that a person becomes 'me'.

P2 Which comes first, commitment or belonging? Can we belong to something we're not committed to? Conversely, can we be committed to something we don't feel we belong to? In many cases the two have to grow together, so that the more we feel we belong, the more committed we become, and the more committed we become, the more we feel we belong.

P3 For many Young Friends, belonging to the Religious Society of Friends is publicly celebrated in membership, and in fact the number of Young Friends who are members has increased as a result of thinking about the issue of commitment for the purposes of this lecture. However, those of us who are attenders are not necessarily any less committed.

P4   What unites us as Quakers? We do not have a monopoly on diversity and tolerance. Nor do we have a monopoly on turning our faith into action. The thing we most obviously share is a form of silent worship, and connected to that, a business method which eschews decisions taken by a majority or even by consensus in favour of a corporate attempt to find the way forward. Both of these rest on the commitment to seeking, within oneself and in others, 'that of God' in everyone.

P5   We tend to subscribe to a particular mode of discontent with the current state of the world. This is especially true of Young Friends. It is almost taken for granted not just that a Quaker supports pacifism, fair trade, the cancellation of third world debt, and any number of environmental issues, but also that such support is rooted in his or her faith. However, an apparent convergence in outlook may mask differences in our fundamental beliefs, or even an absence of them.

P6   In a religious society that respects the individual spiritual paths taken by its members and attenders, testimonies are what unite us. They provide some unity of value and belief, in the way in which silence provides a unity of method.

Testimonies show us the route to follow if we want to reach a particular destination. They may offer a choice of destination or of routes (some more scenic than others!). Above all, they offer the comfortable realisation that a certain route has been travelled before. Testimonies are not simply the common ground that we find in our belief; they are statements of experience, evidence of past witness. This has been profoundly revealed to us in the process of writing this lecture.

If our testimonies are what unite us as Quakers, then they should go beyond mere words and become, if you'll forgive the cliché, a way of life. They are public statements of our commitment. This may have drastic implications: if the world appears less good than it might be in the light of our testimonies, then we must act to change it. It is not just through agreement with the testimonies that we identify ourselves as Quakers, but also through our commitment to upholding them.

P7 If commitment to bringing about positive change in the world is a way of being a Quaker, then Quaker meetings should surely inspire us to do this. If the depth of our concern springs from a spirituality which is unable to tolerate what is unjust or lacking in perspective, then Meeting for Worship is the environment in which that spirit can be encouraged. However, it is not always that way.

Why do some of us leave meeting empowered, while others feel merely satisfied? Is it a problem of the individual meeting or of the individual Quaker? Could it be in the timing of meetings, which seems designed only to fit in with that of church services? How many of us have felt troubled with the world, for whatever reason, all week, only to find ourselves in a comfortable old meeting house surrounded by comfortable old Friends on some pleasant Sunday morning on which the whole world seems to be just right? In short, how can meetings 'release the divine', empowering us to be Quakers?

P8 We carve out our lives through our personal and public statements of commitment and belonging in any number of contexts: our meetings, communities, lifestyles, relationships ... In all aspects of our lives, how can we fulfil our commitments and nurture our sense of belonging in a way that answers 'that of God/godde'?

> If I speak in the tongues of men and angels, but have not love, I am a noisy gong or a clanging cymbal. And if I have prophetic powers, and understand all mysteries and all knowledge, and if I have all faith, so as to remove mountains, but have not love, I am nothing. If I give away all I have, and if I deliver my body to be burned, but have not love, I gain nothing. (1 Corinthians 13, v. 1-3)

Our most important commitment is to faith, hope and, above all, love. Love is the courage we need to uphold our commitment to the things that we believe in. Love is also the gift we receive when we belong. A commitment to the giving and receiving of love empowers our every action and breathes life into our words. Our lives will become living testimonies, and, guided by the living testimony of others, we might more fully take up the entreaty once made by George Fox:

> ... be patterns, be examples in all countries, places, islands, nations, wherever you may come, that your carriage and life may preach among all sorts of people, and to them; then you will come to walk cheerfully over the world, answering that of God in everyone. (Emphasis ours.) (*Quaker Faith and Practice*, 1995, 19.32)

... but who are we to think we might do all this?

P9   We are Young Friends, we are Quakers. We are the here and now, with past witness shaping our identities and a passion for the future informing our ideals.

We are united, we are diverse. We strive to accept ourselves and each other, to nurture, love and answer 'that of God' within.

We are lovers, friends, partners, children, parents, sisters, brothers. We struggle and celebrate, endeavouring to open our hearts to the joy and pain that come with relationships.

We wrestle with apathy and conviction, putting our faith into action and letting our action release sparks of the divine.

Who do we think we are? Through our witness, through our testimony, through our lives, we speak.

Appendix I:
The Road to the Lecture

In February 1996, the Swarthmore Lecture Committee invited Young Friends General Meeting to present the 1998 lecture, taking the theme of 'Commitment and Belonging'. After consideration, YFGM as a whole decided that it should take on the project. We knew that these issues were alive for us, as a group and as individuals. A planning group was appointed to devise a structure and schedule for the task ahead, and to bring the recommendations to the next general meeting in May.

A number of things arose at this early stage:

◆   It was felt to be important that the lecture should be truly a response from Young Friends as a whole, rather than from just a few appointed people on a committee. Therefore the process should involve as many people at as many Young

Friends events as possible.

◆ A small group of people would be needed to steer the whole project through, not necessarily those who would either write or present the lecture itself, but people who would be enthusiastic and committed to seeing the project succeed and would ensure that arrangements were made for the detailed work.

◆ We anticipated that people with many different skills and energies could become involved at various stages in the project, working with a wide variety of media – music, art, video, drama, poetry and so on.

◆ It was recognised that the subject area of commitment and belonging was very wide. We were sure at this stage that there would be plenty to say, but the question remained: how would we focus these subjects into a coherent lecture?

We began by discussing commitment and belonging as concepts. Many of us were eager to discuss ideas and speculation, but we quickly found that it was important to root what we had to say in our own real life experience. It sometimes felt difficult to talk personally about the abstract issues, and it felt at times that there was a lack of focus and little sense of ownership of the subject. We began to look at our own lives in terms of commitment and belonging, and the discourse became less theoretical and much more real as a result.

Throughout 1996, Young Friends talked and wrote about, discussed and played with their ideas around commitment and belonging. In local groups, at the Young Friends Jamboree, at Young Friends National Gathering in Leicester, at European and Middle East Young Friends gatherings in the Netherlands and Brussels, by e-mail with Young Friends around the world and in the pages of Young Quaker magazine – we were exploring the theme and all its possibilities.

We began to discover that the commitments we make and the groups we belong to are an essential element of who we are. They are building blocks in our identity. The issues we cared about were starting to be framed in terms of the 'C'-word and the 'B'-word. The discourse appeared to group naturally into three strongly interrelated areas:

1.   our sense of belonging to the spiritual basis and practice of the Religious Society of Friends;
2.   the ways in which the issues arose in our personal lives between us and our friends, lovers, families; and
3.   our experiences of trying to change the world we live in for the better.

Within these broad areas, we were addressing questions such as these:

1. The Religious Society of Friends
◆   What is our commitment to God?
◆   What is it we can all belong to? How committed are we to the Religious Society of Friends?
◆   What is the basis of our Quakerism? What are the boundaries? What makes someone not a Quaker?
◆   Do we worship God in Meeting for Worship or do we contemplate our lives? Is this the same thing?
◆   Are we searching for Truth if not for God?
◆   In our diversity, is commitment to the Truth what we have in common?

2. Close Relationships
◆   How do we form our own interpretations of changing sexual morality as Friends?
◆   How can we make informed decisions about our sexual

lifestyle and support others who may make different choices?

◆ How do we balance our own needs with those of our chosen and non-chosen families?

3. Social Action

◆ Do we do enough about the issues we feel strongly about?

◆ Do we act more effectively corporately or individually?

◆ Do we have anything new to say about Quaker testimonies?

◆ How essential is integrity of ethics to our lifestyle, and how easily are we swayed from this integrity?

At YFGM in November 1996, we worried that we were trying to cover too much. Were we in danger of trying to say everything and ending up saying nothing? Should we perhaps concentrate on one area, such as Young Friends' position within the Religious Society of Friends? The sense of the meeting shifted again and again. At times we felt completely lost. After much searching, the relevance of the three broad subject areas was rediscovered and we decided to stick with them.

Thus far, it had all been a great deal of hard work, and some were on the verge of despair as to whether the lecture would happen at all or whether we would be able to create something worth presenting. We were told that if we hadn't despaired at times the Swarthmore Lecture Committee would have been 'very worried', as it is an expected, and essential, part of the creative process. It's easy for them to say!

A group of fifteen Young Friends met in January 1997 to compile a synopsis for the lecture, using the written contributions that had been received so far as a basis to work from. For many, it felt like a turning point: there was an injection of new life, new ideas and increased enthusiasm, and it began to feel once again as though the project had the support of the wider body of Young Friends. We decided to focus on the book first as it was due to go to print long before the lecture was to be given. But we still had a number of unresolved issues:

◆ What did Young Friends actually have to say to the rest of Britain Yearly Meeting?
◆ How could we achieve the aims of a Swarthmore Lecture?
◆ What did all we have to say have to do with commitment and belonging?

There seemed to be an infinite number of ways of organising the material we had gathered, and the contributions continued to come, endlessly widening the scope of the subject and deepening the complexity of the interweaving themes. Forming a coherent structure seemed utterly impossible.

The idea of a non-linear, interactive book arose, not so much in response to the problems of organisation, but more as a positive, structural reflection of the contributions, the process and the ownership of the book. It seemed to reflect the fact that, for many Young Friends, the project had become a creative journey, involving challenges and questions. We were all involved in the same process – creating a Swarthmore Lecture on commitment and belonging – yet our own involvement and experiences were unique to every one of us. With a 'living book', we saw that we could extend to each reader the possibility of a similarly unique and creative experience, a different journey for each reader, a different route each time the book is read. The idea was exciting, bold and innovative when compared to previous lectures; the Swarthmore Lecture becoming a game, an adventure – whatever next?!

The written testimonies were so powerful and moving it seemed that little extra narrative would be needed. We decided that all the contributions should be anonymous, with a list of contributors at the end, similar to the 1986 Swarthmore Lecture. The anonymity would perhaps enable some Young Friends to write their contributions more freely, and would also give us a collection of 'I' or 'we' statements that would be easier for the reader to relate to. Two successive editing groups were appointed to collect and collate the contributions, to create the interactive links and questions, and to see the 'book' process through to publication. With continuous feedback, inside and outside of YFGM sessions, the material began to take shape.

Christine Trevett, in her 1997 Swarthmore Lecture, urged Britain Yearly Meeting to start to answer the question 'who do we think we are?' Many Young Friends present were startled – that was the title we had chosen for our 1998 lecture, and we had been addressing that very question for quite some time! Was the 1997 Lecture anticipating our own? It confirmed that YFGM was on the right track and that we had something very meaningful to say to the rest of the Yearly Meeting.

At the time of going to press, the creative process is still in full force: a group has been appointed to oversee the presentation of the lecture, and Young Friends, corporately and individually, are exploring the possibilities that lie ahead. Hundreds of Young Friends have been involved in producing this lecture, both book and presentation. The process has entered our lives in different ways and at different times. We have given different parts of ourselves to the project, enriching it and letting it touch our lives. For many of us, involvement in this creative process has in itself provided acute insight into the nature of commitment and belonging. The themes will continue to be a part of our lives as Young Friends; the process goes on...

Appendix II:
Minutes on Membership (Extracts)

Young Friends were concerned with the issue of membership long before we were invited to give the Swarthmore Lecture on 'Commitment and Belonging'. As testimony to this, the following extracts from a minute of Young Friends Central Committee (YFCC), the body which evolved into Young Friends General Meeting, written in 1990 has been included here.

90/34 Membership Concern
We have discussed the issue of membership of the Society of Friends, a concern which has been brought out by the Friends World Committee for Consultation stipulation that only members should attend the World Conference. When they also express a desire to have 25% of those attending to be Young Friends we see a certain paradox, as many Young Friends are not members, although very involved. This reminded us to consider the broader issue of membership.

As a mixture of members and non-members,

between whom we make no distinction, we felt tolerant of either choice. However, a concern has been expressed that in its present form membership can make attenders feel excluded, and we would wish that by being more sensitive Friends could alleviate this problem. For example, by being more open to non-members attending gatherings and business meetings, or taking on specific responsibilities.

Many Young Friends are committed to the Society of Friends without wishing to become members. This may be because they do not wish to join a seemingly exclusive group or because in the present system of joining a specific local meeting they feel excluded because many of us are fairly itinerant.

Young Friends who, having been brought up in a Quaker family, became members fairly automatically at the age of sixteen, felt they have never had the chance to fully discuss what membership means. Indeed we feel generally an inhibition to talk about spirituality in Quaker circles. If we do want to make a lifelong commitment to the Society of Friends should we not talk and discuss more fully what this means to us on our spiritual journey?

Above all we felt deciding on membership is a personal choice which should be made to express spir-.ituality as well as commitment. If the Society does want to welcome us, it should be for each individual in their own right and what they have to offer.

We, as Young Friends, are glad to come together at an occasion such as YFCC to celebrate each individual's spirituality and the community we form. We find no need to differentiate between those who have attended for longer or shorter periods of time with more or less commitment, but we recognise that each of us has something to give, in whatever way, for however long. Our community flourishes.

We hope to introduce our concern to the Society in general by sending this minute to Meeting for Sufferings, and by requesting that it be published with an introduction in The Friend. It will also be sent to Friends World Committee for Consultation.

After sending the above minute to Meeting for Sufferings in 1991, YFCC received the following in response:

Minute 7: Membership of the Society of Friends

Further to minute 10 of July 1990 we have considered minute 90/34 of Young Friends Central Committee. This has been introduced by Rosie Carnall.

YFCC has found no need to differentiate between those who have been associated with the Society for longer or shorter periods of time but has recognised that each of us has something to contribute. Sometimes membership can make attenders feel excluded. Young Friends who do have a strong sense of spiritual commitment can find the process of applying for membership rather daunting and it can present real problems for someone who is moving around a lot.

We are grateful to have had this matter before us today. We need to be sensitive to all of these issues. Should we be more open to non-members attending gatherings and business meetings or taking on specific responsibilities? The provisions in Church Government paragraph 833 concerning acquisition of membership are extremely flexible and monthly meetings can be imaginative in the way our procedures are used. Membership is the recognition of the spiritual commitment of the Friend.

Appendix III: Contributors

Literally hundreds of people have had a direct or indirect involvement in producing this lecture. They are all, in one way or another, contributors. The written, i.e. tangible, contributions contained in this book represent only the tip of the iceberg. Keeping track of so many names has proved tricky, and the list that follows is inevitably incomplete.

Naomi-Jane Bailey
Jason Barton
Linda Batten
Dawn Beck
Charlee Bewsher
Adam Boulter
Nell Boulton
Jan Brayshaw
Jo Brown
Laura Brown
Gavin Burnell
Leif Burrough
Rowan Burrough
Becky Calcraft

Helen Carmichael
David Carter
Anke Caspers
Jan Caspers
Rachel Clogg
Roger Cookson
Kate Coole
Alex Cooper
Naomi Cordiner
Jane Cowling
Jennie Craddock
John Croh
Fiona Crowther
John Crowther

Alice Drewery
Michael Eccles
Bluebell Eikonoklastes
Chris Elliott
Hannah Engelkamp
Owen Evans
Bryony Evens
Max Evens
Anne Fairweather
Tessa Fairweather
Daphne Fisher
Carolyn Forrest
Ginny Franklin
Andrew Gray

Chris Gribble
Michael Grimes
Nicky Grimes
Anne Haenssgen
Su Hall Jones
Emma Hallet
Zandy Hemsley
Bethan Hillas
Judi Hodgkin
Hanne Høgnestad
Abi Horsfield
Charlotte Hubback
Chris Hunter
Michael Hutchinson
Stephen Inch
Paul Ingram
Karen Inversen
Zeljko Ivankovic
Bee Jasko
Jonathan Kemp
Rachel Kemp
Peter Kennedy
Andrew King
Sally Knowles
Sarah Lambie
Len
Ethel Livermore

Michael Loader
Clare Lockwood
Alice Lynch
Lawrence Martin
Gail Mason
Perdy Matthews
Emily Miles
Will Miles
Geal Fírinne Moran
Alice Morning Star
Pearl-Imogen Morris
Rachel Muers
Edith Mulder
Lindsay Parr
Tony Padget
Robin Pairman
Ben Parker
Nick Perks
Rachel Phillips
Sarah Piercy
Ben Pink Dandelion
Anne Pommier
Wil Quick
Edward Rogers
Heather Rowlands
Dietlind Schreiber
Georg Schwerendt

Marcus Scott
Pen Sennels
Anne Shackleton
Anna Sharman
Cathy Sharman
Jenny Shellens
Ceinwen Silverbrooke
Michael Simpson
Becci Singh
Derek Sloane
Becky Smith
Katy Smith
Sophie Smith
Lana Snook
Michael Stokes
Juliette Stoller
Ruth Strange
Suzanne
Andy Taylor
Katy Turquoise
Paddy Uglow
Gillian Waddilove
William Waddilove
Caroline Webb
Hannah Williams
John Woods
Angela Wylie

Resources

Rape Crisis helplines are in local telephone books.
The London Rape Crisis Centre number is 0171 837 1600.
The Samaritans' number is 0345 90 90 90.
London Lesbian and Gay Switchboard – 0171 837 7324
Bisexual Phoneline – 0181 569 7500
Childline – 0800 1111
Cruse (Bereavement) – 0181 332 7227